Darryl,
Keep changing
my,

LEADING
YOUR
~~CHILDREN~~
PARENTS

25 RULES TO EFFECTIVE
MULTIGENERATIONAL LEADERSHIP
FOR MILLENNIALS & GEN Z

RAVEN SOLOMON

First paperback edition February 2019

Cover design by aksaramantra

Book design by Pankaj Runthala

ISBN 978-1-7336545-0-0 (Paperback)
ISBN 978-1-7336545-2-4 (Hardcover)
ISBN 978-1-7336545-1-7 (eBook)

Published by Raven Solomon Enterprises LLC

www.ravensolomon.com

DEDICATION

To the woman who modeled servant leadership for me before I knew it was "a thing." Without a title, without a certification, you are and forever will be the greatest leader I know. I am only because you were. May you continue to rest in peace knowing that your work was well done.

I love you, Mommy.

CONTENTS

PART THREE

PREFACE

It was 4:30am and my alarm clock was going off. Typically, I'm an avid snoozer, but whenever I'm excited about the day to come, my adrenaline kicks in and I pop up like a jackrabbit. This was one of those days. I was fresh out of college and this was my first real week at my brand-new job. Not only will I finally be able to make some real money but I could apply the four-years-worth of business knowledge I'd crammed in my brain during my time at the prestigious North Carolina State University (Go Pack!). But it didn't go like I'd imagined.

Let's rewind this story a little bit. About two months before, I'd made my family the proudest on the planet by graduating as valedictorian of my class of over 8000 students. All the accolades, the praise, the congratulations and my peers' awestruck looks made me feel on top of the world! With my work ethic and new credentials, I felt like I could do anything, especially professionally. So, during the recruiting phase, it was simply a matter of *what*. Any company would be happy to have the valedictorian of the largest university in North Carolina on their team, right!? It wasn't that I considered myself to be a big shot professional recruit, looking to be a #1 draft pick companies were fighting over. I just considered myself a blessed, hardworking student who had overcome some tremendous odds to walk across the graduating stage, let alone sit on it. I was pretty much grateful to have any company interested in me. I won't lie, it was pretty awesome that there were so many, though.

My major was Business Management with a concentration in Marketing and my minor was Spanish. I received only two B's during my undergrad career, and to this day I can't stand Geology! (The other B was the lab for the class.) Besides the two B's, my grades were A-, A or A+. After two one-week spring break service trips, a semester studying in Mexico and countless hours of coursework, I finally became fluent in Spanish, another stat I knew made me even more marketable.

So, with stellar stats, a few companies in heavy pursuit and my confidence at an all-time high, you're probably wondering what the heck type of job I accepted that had me waking up at 4:30am!? One would likely think I accepted some big-time marketing job at a Fortune 500 Company, or got a full-ride to a Top-10 MBA program to knock out another degree. Both sound awesome, but would be wrong. I chose sales. Sales management, to be exact. This was a choice I questioned every morning when I looked at my alarm clock and it read anything earlier than 5 a.m.! But here's the kicker—I was waking up at that hour to drive a box truck and put up snacks for 10-14 hours. Yes, you read that right. The bilingual valedictorian of North Carolina State University had a manual labor job running a snack route.

I know for a fact you are currently thinking—why the heck and *how* the heck!? The story goes like this:

I was at my third career fair of my graduating semester. I hadn't come across that company or job that made me say *wow* yet. *Wow* about the people, *wow* about the job opportunity and *wow* about the salary. There'd always be at least one missing at each table. That is, until I came across F&B Company. *Wow*...the people were relatable, down-to-earth, and looked like me. *Wow*...the job opportunity sounded absolutely awesome. And *wow*...the salary was *niiiiiiice*. I'd finally found a company on which I didn't have to compromise one of my major three sought-after qualities. There was one downside, however, if you can call it that. I would have to run a chip route for about six-to-eight months.

It was a year-long managerial training program to prepare me to lead a team of frontline route salespeople and merchandisers, manage anywhere from five-million to ten-million in annual sales and manage the relationships with the hundreds of customers who generated those sales. I'd have an office, but most of my responsibility would be out in the field, working with my team, building relationships with my customers and selling. I'd be a district manager right out of college and I'd be paid like one! Doesn't sounds too bad now, does it? Ha-ha!

Believe it or not, this was one of the qualities about the job—and even more so the company—that caught my attention. To me, it showed their dedication to the frontline and the value they put on learning the business from the ground up. I loved the fact that every senior leader in the sales organization had, at some point, run a route. It spoke volumes to me and reminded me of the concept of leadership I'd learned as a hungry sophomore in college that would forever shape my approach to leading—servant leadership. I immediately saw this picture in my head, one I'd seen many times before during my time as a college student.

Figure P.1[1]

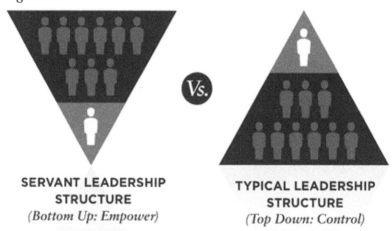

SERVANT LEADERSHIP STRUCTURE
(Bottom Up: Empower)

TYPICAL LEADERSHIP STRUCTURE
(Top Down: Control)

Good ole bottom up leadership!

I'd always been a very compassionate and passionate person, so my introduction to servant leadership was like meeting a soulmate. It put words to what I felt in my heart but could never quite express.

It was the only type of managerial job I wanted—one which gave me the foundation and autonomy to be a servant leader. I'd found my match!

The road wasn't easy. In my mind, I probably quit that job 50 times. The back of those trucks in the 90+ degrees summer days in North Carolina reached well over 100 degrees on most days. The bending, the kneeling, the squatting, the pushing and the pulling was NO JOKE. It was absolutely exhausting tough, physical labor. I put up about hundred cases of chips per day, and on some days several hundred, depending on the route type.

As a woman, there is one week of every month that can be particularly uncomfortable in any job. But running a chip route in the dead of the summer made that time of the month THE WORST! I wish I could sugarcoat that some, but I'd rather just be flat out honest—it sucked! I remember hurling in the bathroom of quite a few stores and popping ibuprofen like Sour Patch Kids in the front seat of the branded metal box that on some days felt like a microwave.

On the frequent occasions I considered walking off the job as a haughty valedictorian probably should have, there were three things that always kept me going: (1) the people, (2) my personal will and (3) the money. (Just being honest!) But I want to talk about the people.

I had a great support system, many of whom had done this before. They believed in me enough to recruit me and heavily hedge their bets on me and I wasn't about to let them down. It was no surprise to the company that this portion of the training program had the potential of running some people off, so they were very intentional about providing us with mentors and other resources to get us through those rough days. There was one friend in particular who should still be sick eight years later, after all the venting I did to her! Those people really helped me through, and I felt I would have been letting them down if I were to quit during the process.

But even more than the support system, I mainly kept going for my future team. As their impending leader, they needed to see me dedicated no matter what. I didn't have to be perfect. I didn't even have to be quick. But what I did have to be was *strong*. This wasn't just a training program for me to learn the business. This was my trial period in their eyes.

Could I withstand the pressure? The heat? The discomfort? Could I do the things I would later be asking them to do?

In many ways they were looking to see if they could trust me as their leader. My personal will is strong, yes, and the money was indeed nice, but nothing fueled me more than proving myself to the people who would soon be calling me *Boss*. I didn't just have to make it through—I had to set the example, despite any and every challenge.

Were they really watching? You bet your bottom-dollar they were! Like a hawk. And they all talked to one another, so if one of them lived near and shopped in a store I serviced, they would check my rotation to see if I was slacking. For that reason, I kept it buttoned up. They would not have a performance reason to not trust me as their leader.

The good news is, I killed the route portion of my training program! And it wasn't because I was great at running routes. I was as slow as molasses. It was because I held myself to a high standard and dedicated myself fully to delivering against it. I worked my butt off and in turn gained the respect of my peers, future subordinates and my superiors, a group I will from now on affectionately refer to as my **PSS**. Those eight months on the route laid the foundation of trustworthiness on which an almost eight-year career of unprecedented progression was built.

Fresh out of college and after participating in a seemingly gruesome managerial training program (it wasn't that bad, I promise), I found myself in charge of a team of experienced adults, most of them old enough to be my parents. (That's where the title of this book comes from, just in case you hadn't caught that yet!) I had a lot of leadership experience through school, but it had all consisted of leading my peers, give or take a few years, or those younger than me. Never had I been responsible for leading people 10-40 years my senior—people literally old enough to be my parents, and even grandparents if they were frisky and got an early start! This was nuts! It sounded awesome on paper to be a District Manager responsible for all of these team members and a high sales volume, but there was something about it in real life that was largely intimidating and nerve-wracking. I remember literally shaking in my boots during my first district meeting.

Just like that night before my first day on the route, I couldn't sleep the night before this meeting either. It wasn't that I didn't know what I was doing. It was that I didn't know *what I was doing*, LOL. I knew business, I knew the numbers and I knew how to communicate and make friends, but I didn't know how to get up there and command the respect of leadership from people who, in theory, should be leading me. People whom I was tempted to call Mr. Robinson instead of Mike. I knew they saw me as *just a kid*, and the truth is, in some ways, I was!

But I had to figure out a way to get over my fears and get them over their doubts. It took time, but I did it. I gained confidence and earned their trust and respect. As it turned out, I was pretty darned good at it.

I went on to lead my first team to District of the Year in our first year together. We weren't together long, as that same trustworthiness led to me being asked to take on a larger district with a larger customer base and bigger responsibility. I obliged, and a few months later received the second promotion of my career. A little over two years later came the next. A year-and-a-half after that, the next. And before I knew it, I found myself sitting in an executive-level position at the ripe old age of 28, one of the youngest to hold such a position nationally. In a $15-billion-dollar organization! I reached my goal of earning a six-figure base salary two years early. I was responsible for hundreds of employees, hundreds of millions of dollars in sales and expenses and thousands of customer relationships. I'd reached the level I'd only dreamed of and knew the trajectory could only continue to be more positive from there. I was on my way to a VP seat faster than I could have believed!

Then 2016 happened. I was diagnosed with epilepsy and needed to make some major life adjustments to get and stay well. I made the tough decision to leave F&B Company in pursuit of something that provided me the new level of work/life balance I needed and the satisfaction of fulfilling part of my life's purpose.

In enters—*YOU!*

I began a career speaking to and coaching students, young professionals and emerging leaders to overcome obstacles and thrive. Part of my coaching consists of helping Millennials and Gen Zers, defined in Chapter 1, navigate their careers in corporate America and the other part consists of helping other generations better understand and leverage the Millennial and Gen Z talent within their influence. As I began communicating with all three populations I just described, I started to notice a clear unreadiness in the Millennial population as it related to leading in business and corporate America. There seemed to be a gap between Millennials' preparation for leadership and the competencies needed by companies in effective leaders.

Much of the feedback I received was that the knowledge of Millennials coming out of college was superb. Their book sense was strong. But the managerial maturity and leadership-readiness was not there. And the disparity was causing frustration on the both ends.

How do we close the gap?

In enters—ME!

I was able to strike a balance in my career of *change agent* and *respecter-of-past-practices* that led to my gaining the trust and respect of my peers, subordinates and superiors (PSS's), which took me to great heights. Some may think it's an art, but I've taken the time to convert it into a science.

In enters—*THIS BOOK*!

Here is your readiness guide to becoming effective Millennial and/or Gen Z leaders of multigenerational teams. This book is going to show you exactly how to gain **and keep** the trust and respect of your PSS's, so you can be the rock-star leader of your parents you have the knowledge to be!

INTRODUCTION

Welcome, you future (or current) young professional, you! If you've cracked open this book, it means you are preparing for or recently stepped into the workplace and have some desire to be a leader within it. Well, good news...you've picked the right book! Whether you're in a managerial training program that promises you some sort of leadership role at the end or you're in an individual contributor role and just want to be a successful employee, this book will help prepare you to lead and thrive as a young professional in a multigenerational environment.

And the truth is, you need it, right?! Not because you're incapable of figuring out this transition from college to the professional world on your own but because the workplace is a very different and slightly intimidating place than the one you are leaving or just left.

For the past several years, you've been in an environment pretty much created for you. The training, the leaders, the staff, the programs, the buildings, the culture and even the food were all created with you in mind. They existed to be in service to you.

11

Partially because you're so special, as I'm sure you believe, but mainly because you were **the customer**. Just like any other business, the customers are the focal point and the basis of most decisions.

Your workplace, the professional world, is quite different. It was not created with you in mind, does not exist in sole service to you and when you arrive, you will not be the customer. You'll be introduced to new training, new styles, new leaders, new staff, new programs, new buildings and most importantly, a new culture, all of which you will be responsible for acquainting yourself with and navigating to produce desired results in your role. Sounds like a pretty big transition to me, wouldn't you say?

It is such a large transition that you might expect there to be droves of resources out there to aid in this transition, but there are surprisingly few. Frankly, I found none specifically focused on helping you, a recent college graduate, navigate this complex multigenerational workplace in the tech-driven world we live in today.

Furthermore, I found 10 x 0 (that's still zero) resources out there to help you LEAD effectively in said workforce. This, my friend, was my sole motivation in writing this book. There just isn't much out there to guide you through the transition from student life to professional life. From student leadership to workplace leadership. From working almost solely with people your age to now working with people twice your age. I know the pain with which you will soon become acquainted and I want to mitigate it—one page at a time.

When dreaming of this book, I imagined a how-to guide for young professionals like yourself that can be picked up multiple times throughout your career— at the beginning of your career, the moment you take over your first team and again when you begin leading your first team of leaders. I wanted it to be easy to read, follow and navigate. I wanted a cool cover, because we Millennials are pretty visual, but I wanted its contents to be 20 times cooler.

For that reason, I spent a year-and-a-half writing it. I wanted to include all the lessons I learned as a budding professional, either from the mistakes I made, the things I did well that were rewarded or the mistakes/wins I saw others make. I chose carefully the most relevant and important 25 Rules I learned to follow throughout the first eight years of my corporate career—the rules that led me to an executive-level job at one of the largest food and beverage companies in the world at 28-years-old, leading a 200+ team of employees and a $200MM+ annual business. These are the rules that separated me from my peers and led to CEO recognition, countless high-potential leadership development programs and consistent business and people results. The rules that prepared me for my unexpected transition to entrepreneurship after battling illness, and the very things I noticed separating those employees being promoted from those who weren't.

The 25 Rules I share with you in the pages to come are important for leading in the workplace, but they are equally important for engaging with people in general, inside and outside of the workplace.

Can I guarantee you'll end up with similar results as I had if you follow all 25 of these rules to the T? Of course not. There are far too many factors involved. However, I can guarantee you will be more prepared to handle the complexities of the multigenerational workplace, understand what it takes to be an effective leader of a multigenerational team and have a set of tools to use as you navigate your first few years of professional leadership. I can guarantee answers to questions like:

- What do I need to know that college probably hasn't taught me?

- What mindset do I need to have entering the workforce and interacting with what may soon be my team of employees?

- What skills do I need to strengthen and why?

- What should be my personal objectives when entering my new environment in order to be most successful?

- And so much more...

To be clear, this book is about leadership. It is ideally written for the young professional who is about to embark upon leading their first team, which is likely multigenerational. However, as I teach in one of my workshops, *leading* can be done without position or title. Learning to lead people despite you position or title is one of the best skills you can sharpen stepping into the workplace. Please, please, please do not think you need a title to benefit from the contents of this book.

THE STRUCTURE

I want you to think of this book as your *cheat sheet* to a successful transition from college to leadership in the professional world. This cheat sheet tells you what you need to do **before** stepping into the multigenerational workplace to lead your multigenerational team, rules to follow **while** you lead your multigenerational team and important things to do **outside** of leading your team while you lead your team. Following this thought process, I've broken the book into three sections:

1) **Before the Job:** Rules for Preparing to Lead Your Multigenerational Team

2) **On the Job:** Rules for Leading Your Multigenerational Team

3) **Around the Job:** Rules for Leading Effectively Outside of Your Multigenerational Team

Before the Job: Rules for Preparing to Lead Your Multigenerational Team

Before you step into your new role as a leader of a multigenerational team (and a hungry individual contributor, as we've discussed), there are a few important things you need to know—a few important rules to keep in mind. The first is making sure you don't fall for the HR Pickup Line. The second is to really understand the values of other generations in the workplace, and the last is to understand the different communication styles/preferences by generation.

Understanding these rules and following them will help prepare you for the many rules you'll need to practice on the job.

These rules will open your mind to an important perspective.

On the Job: Rules for Leading Your Multigenerational Team

There are several rules you should abide by once you begin leading your team, and this section covers those in depth. It ranges from admitting you don't know everything, to how to make a proper introduction to your team, to following up and holding your team accountable. You'll want to revisit this section right before you take over your new team.

These rules get you results.

Around the Job: Rules for Leading Effectively Outside of Your Multigenerational Team

Being a leader in the workplace doesn't start or end with the team for which you are responsible. It is just as much about how you lead around the office as it is about how you lead within your team. This, however, you probably haven't heard much about.

This section is arguably the most important section of the book, not because the others aren't important, but because these are probably the rules least talked about. You're likely not going to find these spelled out anywhere around your workplace, but they are absolutely the issues many promotional decisions are made around and from which judgement is cast. It'd be safe to call these the

Unwritten Rules—they are expected and implied but rarely ever explained.

These rules get you promoted. **Secret:** They are contingent upon mastery of the other two sets.

Hashtags

This book is centered around *soft skills*—essential people skills necessary to effectively connect with, engage with and lead people. They include both intrapersonal and interpersonal skills and are sometimes referred to as *emotional intelligence*, but frankly encompass more. On the contrary, hard skills are the technical expertise and knowledge needed to perform a job or task. As you can imagine, hard skills are easier to measure and easier to learn due to their objective nature, while soft skills are more subjective, hence their name, and can be more difficult to assess. Both are important, but is one more important than the other? To answer that question, I would say this—hard skills get you hired and soft skills get you promoted. These days, being technically capable is what gets your foot in the door to compete. They are vital to do the job—and that's important. But, soft skills are what enable you to win. They take your performance to the next level, making you a more valuable employee and leader.

In today's collaborative, team-oriented workplace, soft skills are more important now than they ever were. The World Economic Forum, a global, not-for-profit organization committed to improving the state of the world by engaging business, political, academic and other leaders of society to shape global, regional and industry agendas, listed in their Future of Jobs[1] reports the top-ten desired skills for 2020 as:

10. Cognitive Flexibility

9. Negotiation Skills

8. Orientation to Service

7. Decision Making and Judgement

6. Emotional Intelligence

5. Coordinating with Others

4. People Management

3. Creativity

2. Critical Thinking and

1. Complex Problem Solving

100% of these skills fall into or directly relate to soft skills.

Publication after publication, article after article, continuously cite soft skills as the essential skills for the current and future workplace, yet the soft skill capabilities of the Millennial and Gen Z generations seems to be declining. You and I are lacking the skills of the future. Why? Many accredit it to that handheld device which is likely no more than five-feet away from you as you read this book. Because we are so technologically proficient, and in some cases dependent, we spend a lot less time interacting with people outside of screens as prior generations have. With that comes a lack of proficiency in face-to-face human connection and even developed anxiety. Some studies have shown a correlation between the social anxiety of face-to-face interactions with the amount of online interactions one participates in. Simply put, the more time a participant spent on his or her phone, the less comfortable he or she was in face-to-face situations.[2] Our Baby Boomer parents had no Facetime or text messaging, so they spent all their people time actually talking via phone or in person.

Regardless of the cause, managers and hiring managers in the workplace find soft skills to be harder to find or are underdeveloped in our generations.

According to a 2016 Workforce-Skills Preparedness Report done jointly by PayScale, Inc., a compensation data and software provider, and Future Workplace, an executive development firm, 87% of new college graduates feel well-prepared for their job upon graduation. That's great, except for the fact that only about half of their managers agree. In this survey, only half of hiring managers felt their recent-college-graduate employees were well-prepared for the workforce. The crucial skills they said these employees lacked? Mostly soft-ish skills—critical thinking, attention to detail, communication, business writing, leadership, and public speaking.[3]

Unless you are a communications or social studies major, most of your coursework in college was probably taught to strengthen your hard skills—your technical prowess in a given subject matter. You've spent plenty of time sharpening the hard skills necessary to get to this level. For that reason, I want this book to focus solely on the soft skills you'll need to be successful. So, I've #hashtagged it for you!

I'm almost certain I don't need to explain what a hashtag is, so I won't insult your coolness by trying to do so. I'll simply tell you how they work in this book—the same way hashtags are used in the world of social media. Each chapter has a set of soft skills which are hashtagged on its opening page. In the index at the back of this book, you'll find every soft skill captured throughout the pages. Anytime you need to quickly access information about a certain soft skill, flip to the back of the book to be directed to the rules you'll need to follow to display that soft skill.

For example, let's say you receive feedback that you are inconsistent in your accountability. Your team is receiving different levels of discipline from you for similar mistakes/offenses. After the initial shock wears off, you pick up this book, knowing you will find some guidance to changing that behavior. You flip to the index looking for #accountability. The index points you to *Rule #9: Be Consistent* and *Rule #11 Follow Up and Follow Through*. You reread those chapters and are reminded of why consistency is so important and what behaviors you need to change to begin demonstrating them now.

The purpose of the hashtags is to make it easy to find turnkey direction for your circumstances on the spot. You'll be busy in your new role, so I want you to have a quick and simple resource at your disposal.

Now that you understand the framework of the book, let's jump right in! Remember, this was written with you and the success of your career in mind. Immerse yourself in it and watch you and your team grow.

UNDERSTANDING THE GENERATIONS

#empathy
#interpersonalskills
#selfawareness
#diversityawareness

You may or may not have heard this stat, but there are quite possibly more generations working alongside each other in the workplace than ever before. The moment one exits, another enters. If age itself doesn't already create enough of a gap, the speed at which technology moves in today's world makes generational gaps seemingly wider than they were in the past, adding even more complexity. Allow me to explain using the telephone as an example.

There were right around 100 years between the invention of the first telephone and the first cellular telephone. While it looked very different and grew in terms of quality, think about it—four generations grew up with the same level of communicative technology. For all my late Millennials and Gen Z members, it looked a little something like this—If you wanted to speak to someone who was physically in a different location than you, you located a phone connected to a physical telephone line and you dialed a number, albeit in different ways, to connect with that person. That person, too, had to be in a location where a physical telephone line existed and was connected to the number you dialed. If they weren't available, you simply missed the call and they had no way of knowing you'd called them. Voicemail came along in 1973 (almost 100 years after the telephone was invented) and about 10 years later, Caller ID became available for households.

Also in 1973, the first cellular phone was invented and completely blew the minds of those growing up and working during that time. Baby Boomers, likely your parents or grandparents, were between 9 and 17 years of age at the time the cell phone was introduced. Just like the introduction of any new and groundbreaking technology, it was expensive at first and most working-class families couldn't afford one. The average Boomer probably didn't own a cell phone until around the mid to late 80s. Fast forward only 19 years after the first cellular phone we were introduced to the invention of the first smartphone.

Today, 46 years after the first cell phone was introduced, a generation who grew up in a time where cell phones didn't even exist are now expected to hold what is basically a mini computer in their hand, send short letters that deliver almost instantaneously (email or text messages) and talk "face-to-face" via a screen, as in the futuristic cartoon they remember seeing as kids and teenagers—

The Jetsons. As the evolution of the telephone demonstrates for us, technological advancements are being made in half the time it used to take. Someone born in the 50s must make considerable effort to "keep up" as compared to past generations. The gap widens and the effort to close it is greater.

In order to make that example and set the stage for our conversation about the different generations, I realize I pretty much jumped right in, assuming you knew what a generation is and how each generation working in our workplace is defined.

DEFINING A *GENERATION*

Why don't we start by discussing what a *generation* truly is. We use the word all the time, but if you're anything like I was prior to entering this line of work, you've probably never thought about what is really means and why.

Simply stated, a generation is all the people born and living at about the same time, regarded collectively.[1] My friends at Gen HQ call it a group of people born around the same time and raised around the same place, because they believe location matters.[2] Generally speaking, you and I know this definition of the word *generation*. The deeper question is *what makes a generation a generation*, aside from when they were born and where they live? The best answer to this question, I believe, is from LifeCourse Associates[3] a company built by some of today's leading generationalists and authors of one of my favorite books about the subject—**Generations** (1991). It is an aggregate of perspectives from two centuries of some of the most astute generational writers in the world. *LifeCourse* notes that a generation has three criteria:

1. Share an age location in history. They encounter key historical events and social trends while occupying the same phase of life.

2. Share some common beliefs and behaviors, including basic attitudes about risk taking, culture and values, civic engagement and family life.

3. Have a sense of common perceived membership in that generation. Most members of various generations identify themselves as a unique group with a different outlook from those outside their generation.

Because I'm a millennial, I'll use my generation to provide examples of these criteria. My millennial peers and I were all born between 1980 and 1995. We experienced social trends together, like the onset of social media and the infiltration of hip-hop culture into fashion in new ways. We remember FUBU, Phat Farm, Myspace, Friendster and the days when Facebook was only for college students. We remember being in school (some high-school, some middle-school and some even college) when 9/11 happened. We saw airport security change nearly overnight. As a generation, bombs in public places was our biggest security fear and although order generations experienced these same events, our experience at this particular phase of our lives gives us a shared perspective.

Generally speaking, we Millennials value experiences over things. We're slower to buy homes and settle down to have a family because we value the creation of memories and want the flexibility of creating them. We were raised by helicopter parents and, of course, received participation trophies growing up, so we're super confident, optimistic and like consistent feedback on our performances. These are just a few of the common beliefs, values and basic attitudes we share as Millennials.

Lastly, we naturally believe that our generation is unique from everyone else's. We say things like, "This generation will never know what blowing your Nintendo cartridge is like." Or, "This generation doesn't appreciate playing outside." Or how about this one— "This is not real music!" However, you've probably heard your elders say things like this, as well. They, too, have a sense of pride in how they grew up, the things they had, the things they did and the memories they created. Every generation thinks the music of their time is "real music." Every generation has a sense of common perceived membership.

Now that we have an understanding of what a *generation* is, let's take a look at each generation and some respective truths.

THE GENERATIONS

I should start by saying there is no governing body which determines when a generation technically starts and when it ends. If you Googled *generations by year,* you'll probably notice that different sources have different start and end years for generations, typically within one-to-four years. That's because there is not one authority which establishes the years or names of a generation, so demographers and generational experts—and to some extent culture—define these things over time.

We should also note that the below categorizations and descriptions of each generation are just that—categorizations. They don't apply to every member of that generation and these generalizations describe trends across the collective.

My last disclaimer is that generations are less about age and more about experiences and the beliefs and behaviors often shaped by those experiences. For example, a Millennial raised by grandparents or older parents tend to think and behave more like a Gen Xer than the average Millennial. I'd probably be a good example of that, being raised partially by my grandmother and partially by my mother. People tell me all the time I'm not your "typical Millennial" and I credit that back to being raised under a more Traditionalist value system as opposed to Baby Boomer, particularly in my formative years.

Enough with the disclaimers. Let's jump into a quick, high-level overview of the five most prevalent generations today. They breakout as such:

Table U.1

	BORN IN	AGE IN 2019
Traditionalists (Silent Generation)	1925 - 1945	74 - 94
Baby Boomers	1946 - 1964	55 - 73
Gen X	1965 - 1979	40 - 54
Millennials (Gen Y)	1980 - 1995	24 - 39
Gen Z (iGen, Centennials)	1996 - 2012	6 - 23

Traditionalists

These are likely your great-grandparents or, depending on how old you are when you read this book, maybe even great-great-grandparents. They were born between 1925 and 1945, give or take a few years on both ends. Because they are no longer in the workplace, generally speaking, we'll spend very limited time discussing them, but I will include them now to provide a little context for understanding the generations that follow.

Also referred to as the Silent Generation, Traditionalists were children of both the Great Depression and World War II. Growing up in such an economic downturn and global unrest, as adults, they were risk-averse, disciplined and conforming. They grew up in a time where children were seen and not heard, meaning they respected their elders and the powers that were and they didn't have a voice as a child.

Some of their values consist of hard work, dedication, respect for rules, honor, patriotism and loyalty. When speaking of work, age equals seniority.

Popular Traditionalists you may know: Martin Luther King Jr., Former Vice President Joe Biden, Elvis Presley, Ray Charles, Former Senator John McCain and Senator Bernie Sanders.

Baby Boomers

Depending on whether you are a Millennial or Centennial, these are likely your parents or grandparents. They were born between 1946 and 1964, give or take a few years on both ends, and get their namesake from the baby boom which occurred after World War II, for which many theories exist to try and explain.

When Baby Boomers were children, one of the bloodiest wars of all time had ended, the U.S. economy was recovering from the depression and families were more optimistic than ever about the future. This environment made for a very different experience growing up for Baby Boomers than for Traditionalists. This difference, amongst others, made Boomers fairly optimistic. They had a much more pleasant upbringing, had been sold the American Dream and felt comfortable rebelling against conformity and questioning authority and the play-by-the-rules mentality of their predecessors.

Some of the most memorable events and cultural influences for Baby Boomers include the mass influx of women entering the workforce, the first American on the moon, the civil rights movement, suburban living, the Vietnam War, the Hippie Movement and the Sexual Revolution.

When it comes to work, Baby Boomers live to work. Similar to their predecessors, hard work is one of their core values and they believe in working your way to the top by *paying your dues.* Baby Boomers can be workaholics defined by their careers and value visibility (facetime) at work. They often, therefore, lack a work-life balance—the balance between work and personal life. Money, title and recognition are important to them and denotes success in the workplace. They are competitive, idealistic and seek personal growth and personal gratification but can also be very team-oriented. Conflict is not their thing, and despite their questioning of authority, they respect the workplace hierarchy and tend to follow protocol tightly. They believe long hours show commitment, they are politically sensitive and can also be sensitive to feedback. We will revisit some of this later in the two chapters to follow as we consider how these characteristics about Boomers and the generations to follow shape our interaction with members of our teams who are of that generation.

Popular Baby Boomers you may know: Formers Presidents Barack Obama and Bill Clinton, Oprah Winfrey, Bill Gates, Steve Jobs, Denzel Washington, Stevie Wonder, Bono and Madonna.

Gen X

Depending on whether you are a Millennial or Centennial, these are likely your parents, young aunts and uncles or older cousins.

They were born between 1965 and 1979, give or take a few years on both ends. (I'm sure you get that point by now.) They are the smallest of the four prominent generations in the U.S. today.

Dubbed as *latchkey kids*, Xers grew up in an interesting time. Societal norms were shifting, divorce rates and maternal participation in the workforce were at all-time highs, and adult supervision, as a result, was lower than it had been in past years. As a result, Xers are super-independent, adaptive and pragmatic. Likely due to how they grew up, Xers enjoy spending lots of time with their children, whom they often treat like friends. What they felt like they missed as kids, they want to give to their own children.

Some of the most memorable events and cultural influences for Gen X include the emergence of MTV, believe it or not, gaming systems like the Game Boy, desktop computers and the normalization of single-parent homes.

When it comes to work, Xers work to live, contrary to their Baby Boomer predecessors. They are also not as loyal to a company as boomers were. Instead, they look at career security versus job security, asking questions of themselves like, "What next step will better serve my career, not just the company?" They value fun, informality, diversity, self-reliance and personal time. They want work/life balance *now*, not later, and unlike their Boomer predecessors, they don't attribute much to long hours. They're all about productivity and efficiency when it comes to doing work and are outcome-oriented and output-focused. Similar to the way they approach their relationship with their kids, they respond to leadership best when it's informal and friendly, until a strong hand is required.

They don't do well with rigid work requirements and appreciate autonomy and trust. Gen X is actually very techno-literal and enjoy working with the latest technology. Their informal default makes them view leadership through an *everyone is the same* lens where anyone can be challenged and asked the question *why* to enhance processes and business results.

Popular Gen Xers you may know: Michael Jordan, Jennifer Lopez, Sandra Bullock, Tiger Woods, Ryan Seacrest, Tom Cruise and J.K. Rowling.

Millennials

You, my friend, might actually fall into this category, depending on when you were born. Millennials, also known as Gen Y, were born between 1980 and 1995, give or take a few years on both ends, and have been given a bad rap, much of which can be explained.

Millennials grew up in a very child-centric society where their *helicopter parents* pretty much made it all about them. Yes, Millennials were the first generation to receive the infamous *participation trophy* as children, forming their sense of entitlement, many believe. They were the first generation of kids who had schedules—school every day, cheerleading practice on Monday, dance on Tuesday, church on Wednesday, basketball practice on Thursday and play group on Saturday. Parents became taxi drivers and were okay with it.

Like their boomer parents, they are optimistic—growing up during a time of relatively stable and positive economic conditions—and idealistic in their desire to change the world. They were sold on the idea they could be anything they wanted and could do anything to which they put their minds. For that reason, they are confident almost to a fault sometimes and achievement-oriented. They are socially conscious, very tech savvy, civic-minded and value experiences over things.

Some of the most memorable events and cultural influences for Millennials include the introduction of social media, school shootings, the Iraq War, 9/11, Hurricane Katrina and mounds of student-loan debt.

When it comes to their philosophy on work, Millennials want to live, then work. As mentioned, their value for experiences and things make them sacrifice the new car and the new home for work/life balance, travel and creating memories with friends. At work, they value collaboration, achievement, a sense of meaning, work/life balance, flexibility and diversity. They are cause-driven and desire to work where they are able to make a difference. They are outcome-driven, not process driven. They are ambitious multitaskers who are entrepreneurial-spirited. They have high expectations of their leaders to mentor them, provide feedback regularly and help them reach their professional goals. The helicopter parenting they experienced as children creates a need for constant feedback and affirmation from their managers.

Just like Xers, Millennials are career-focused, not company-focused. They are less loyal even than the Xers are, seeking both success in their personal and career goals and true meaning in their work. Contrary to popular belief, Millennials aren't anti-hard work—they simply want to work when and where they choose. Where they find both, they can be extremely loyal. As we mentioned at the beginning of this book, many Millennials lack soft skills and need high supervision/ structure around people challenges in the workplace.

Popular Millennials you may know: Beyoncé, Prince William, LeBron James, the Olsen Twins, Kim Kardashian, Ashton Kutcher, Serena Williams and Mark Zuckerberg

Gen Z

Many of you reading this book likely fall into this category. Centennials, more commonly known as Gen Z or iGen these days, were born between 1996 and 2012, give or take a few years on both ends, and soon to be the largest living generation in the U.S.

Gen Z doesn't know a time without the existence of the Internet, some form of social media and smartphones. They are what we call *digital natives* and are frankly tech-dependent. The immediate access to information they have through technology makes them the smartest generation, at their age, to ever live. Thanks also to technology, they are "always on," accept new ideas very easily and are the multitaskers of all multitaskers.

They've watched their older Millennial siblings rack up mounds of debt from college, come back home to live with mom and dad into their adult years and get an incredibly negative reputation in society. Therefore, they are making bipolar-opposite decisions around things like money management and post-secondary education. In greater numbers than ever before, Gen Z will consider non-traditional paths to career success, like trade schools, certifications, skill-based learning programs, etc. Some may even come to an employer with self-taught skills they learned by watching people on the Internet.

Some of the most memorable events and cultural influences for Gen Z include the Great Recession, the rise of ISIS, cyberbullying, Facetime, police shootings and the Black Lives Matter movement.

To date, Gen Zers haven't spent much time in the workplace. But we can infer much from what we see of them in culture, society and education. We know that Gen Z is self-taught and prefers to try to figure things out on their own first and receive guidance from their leaders than to be instructed in more traditional ways. Unlike Millennials, Gen Z seems to be more driven by things than experiences. Financial security is their #1 career aspiration over doing their dream job. They actually prefer face-to-face interaction over text or email and are more independent than collaborative, desiring to be judged by their own merits. Similar to Baby Boomers, they are very competitive. They will be more private than Millennials, as their Gen X parents are far more acquainted with the internet and have taught them what is appropriate for public access and what is not. Like Millennials, they seek meaning in their work. As they seek to be more stable than their Millennial predecessors, we anticipate them making more conservative decisions even in their pursuit of meaningful work.

Popular Gen Zers you may know: Jaden Smith, Kylie Jenner and Shawn Mendes.

THEY NEED YOU

In case you haven't heard, there are lots and lots of Baby Boomers, people born approximately between the years 1946 and 1964, in the United States. Prior to the Millennial, and now Centennial generation, Baby Boomers made up the largest generation the U.S. had ever seen, thanks to the influx in childbearing after the end of World War II. At one time, Baby Boomers made up well over 50% of the U.S. workforce.

However, as the years go by, Boomers are, of course, growing older and are approaching retirement. Imagine over 40 million employees leaving the U.S. workforce across all levels of organizations. Who will fill the jobs they leave behind? Naturally, one would think the generation behind them, which makes a ton of sense. However, unlike their predecessors, the Traditionalists didn't bear as many children, making the generation behind Boomers—Gen X—much smaller. In fact, Gen X is about 3/4 the size of the Baby Boomer generation.[4] Sheer math tells us there is not enough Gen X talent to backfill Boomers as they exit the workplace and jog into retirement.

Which means… ? You got it…there's more room for you!

With Boomers trading in mid-level and senior-level managements positions for seven a.m. walks on the beach and weekday play dates with the grands, there are vacancies requiring Gen X leaders to step into higher roles at younger ages, thus leaving room for Millennials, and now Gen Zers, to step into the leadership roles which would likely be occupied by Gen X, if they were a large enough group. In other words, the mass exodus of Baby Boomers from the workplace due to retirement creates two truths important to you:

- Workplace leaders are getting younger
- There is a particular high demand for young, capable leaders in the workplace

That's right, companies are seeking recent and soon-to-be graduates with leadership capabilities they can train and put into leadership positions at younger ages than ever. See, the mass exodus I've talked about hasn't quite happened yet, but simple math tells us it is near. In order to ensure they have a pipeline of talent ready to fill open positions caused by the exodus, companies are taking young professionals with potential and expediting their development.

An easier way to say it is THEY NEED YOU. Yes, *you*! A smart, hungry, capable young graduate who is humble, willing to learn and able to lead. You'll be around for a while and they need you to carry forth the mission and vision of the organization. Knowing you'll bring ideas and fresh perspective to do it more efficiently via the use of technology makes the deal even sweeter!

The reality is, you are light years smarter than them when they were your age and I believe that most Boomers and Xers get that.

As mentioned before, whether you're a Millennial or a Zer, you are a part of the largest or the soon-to-be largest generation in the U.S. today. The workplace HAS to listen to you. You have great influence as consumers and will soon have great influence as employees and leaders. You, my friend, have all the ingredients necessary to be a FORCE. If you can simply get these leadership essentials right—these *soft skills* right—you will be unstoppable. They need you…and you need this.

YOU NEED THIS

I mean this with as much love as possible. We've kind of hit on it already but I want to share one more source of data with you to backup my claims. If you are not already convinced, hopefully this will convince you. Future Workplace, an executive-development firm dedicated to rethinking and reimagining the workplace, in partnership with Beyond, the Career Network.[5] conducted a 5771-person survey on multigenerational leadership in the workplace in 2015. They study found that:

- 83% of respondents have seen Millennials managing Gen X and Baby Boomers in their office
- 44% of Millennial respondents view themselves as being the most capable generation to lead in the workplace, but only 14% of all survey respondents agree with this sentiment.

- 51% of all respondents feel that Gen X employees are the most capable generation to lead organizations
- 89% of respondents said that building strong leadership skills is important to them, but only 47% work for companies that have a formal mentorship program to support their leadership development

This is where a book like this becomes vital. Reading the book is you investing in self-directed learning which will make you an impactful, multigenerational leader in the workplace.

So, have I convinced you this book is indeed worth your money, time and attention? Great! What do you say we hop into these rules, then, shall we?

PART ONE:

BEFORE THE JOB

Rules for Preparing to Lead
Your Multigenerational Team

RULE #1: DON'T FALL FOR THE HR PICKUP LINE

#discernment

#maturity

#selfmanagement

If your resume is hot enough and your degree fat enough, chances are you heard the HR pickup line at some point during the recruiting or company orientation process. You know exactly what I'm talking about—that famous line which is bound to make any passionate young graduate feel like they've found The One. The line that makes you want to drop every side company you've been stringing along and finally put a ring on it. The ever so captivating:

> *We really want our employees to bring their whole selves to work.*

"Really? My whole self? Sweet!" you probably say to yourself as you walk out of the interview with hearts in your eyes like the in-love emoji.

Before I bash, let me be clear—I think many companies genuinely desire to have a company culture which is respectful and accepting of all cultures, norms, beliefs, values, thought processes and weekend leisurely activities. But the truth is (a) we are not there as a society and (b) as long as work is work, there are certain things which are simply unacceptable for the workplace. It's important to know this as you enter the workforce.

Those *things* include but are not limited to: religion, beliefs on sexual orientation, gender views, limited views on cultural/racial differences and offensive comments on ability/disability. Pretty much any basis covered under Equal Employment Opportunity Act. It may seem limiting but talking about this stuff with the wrong person can get you in a heap of trouble, formally and informally.

For example, let's say you grew up in a very religious home. You and your family are devout in your faith and hold certain beliefs around same-sex marriage. According to your belief system, being gay is wrong. While this might be your opinion, which you are entitled to, it is not inclusive or workplace appropriate to impose or make business decisions based upon it. It likely does not align with the core values of the organization, where hopefully everyone is welcome. If bringing this ideal to work is a deal breaker for you, you may want to work for a company where the leadership shares similar beliefs and the organizational values align with yours.

Let's lighten the mood a little with another example. It's Friday night and you and a couple of your girlfriends go out and have a drunken night on the town. So drunk that you wake up in an unknown place, with unfamiliar people, completely unaware of what happened the night before. You check your phone and go to your **public** Facebook page, which we will discuss a little more in a later chapter, only to find inappropriate pictures of you for all to see.

Now is probably a good time to note that your definition of inappropriate and your *organization's* definition of inappropriate are likely two different things. Not to mention the varying definition of your team members, which only further complicates your life. Always err on the side of caution and go with the conservative version of what you believe your organization's version of inappropriate is.

Anyway, discussing these festivities at work might seem tempting, given you often go to happy hour with coworkers and consider a few of them friends, but trust me, it's not workplace appropriate. And you CERTAINLY shouldn't be sharing any of this with your team members or their peers. This is a part of Self we DON'T want to bring to work. The organization doesn't want it either, trust me!

So what do they mean by "bring your whole self to work," then!? It's mostly about creating an inclusive environment in which every employee feels comfortable enough to contribute through their unique differences, shaped by their diverse experiences. For example, the way you contribute may be completely different than the way I contribute, in the same role, based solely on the distinctive way we communicate, which stems from where we grew up. Someone from Europe may have a completely different construct of work-life balance than you and I do as Americans, but the company goal is to make us all comfortable and productive in our different approaches to getting work done.

There will be times when going a little deeper on your personal values and belief systems are more appropriate than others. One of the key characteristics of a mature leader is being able to discern those times from others. For example, an Employee Resource Group meeting is much more suitable for sharing your opinions on an ethical topic than a sales meeting, or even happy hour afterward. You must always be cognizant of your audience and accurately assess the conversational environment before you speak. To assess the environment, you should consider three things:

1. The **Room** - Who is in the room?

2. The **Discussion** - What is being discussed? Is it workplace appropriate?

3. Your **Stakeholders** - How might my addition to the discussion make my stakeholders feel? My stakeholders are my team, my peers, mentors/sponsors and my boss.

Asking yourself these three questions will save you from a heap of trouble and brand surgery in the future.

Hopefully the next time, or first time, you hear that sexy HR pick-up line—to bring your whole self to work—you're able to decipher what it means and understand how to apply it. Don't believe it and most certainly don't do it! You and I both know if you really brought your whole self, and I mean your WHOLE self to work, there would likely be no more *work* for you to go to! Me too!

RULE #2: VALUE THEIR VALUES

#empathy
#sensitivity
#socialawareness

Whether you are preparing to lead a team or simply work amongst one, the likelihood that it will consist of multiple generations is quite high, especially if you are working anywhere outside of a startup. As we reviewed in the introduction, each generation has its own unique set of experiences, thus characteristics and values. Understanding the different values of the generations sharing in your work environment or in your team will be vital as you attempt to build rapport, gain their respect and earn their trust.

Given my background in sales, I tend to think with a sales cap on. In sales, whenever you are trying to make headway with a client, you start by doing your research to understand what matters most to them. Once you understand that, which is much easier said than done, you then figure out how to position what you offer against what matters most to them and further, what they need. You learn to speak their language in order to effectively communicate what you have that can solve their problems...and yours, for that matter. Preparing to lead your team should be the same as preparing for a sales call. You want to consider what matters most to your team or workgroup so that you're able to position yourself as a leader accordingly.

Let's take a look at what matters generationally for your soon-to-be multigenerational team members—their values—generally speaking, and some ways you can demonstrate those values to best build rapport, gain respect and earn trust.

BABY BOOMERS

Professionally speaking, Baby Boomers have some, what we would likely call, old school values. However, you'll likely find some commonalities as we walk through their top three values that impact how they show up in the workplace.

Hard work

In a nutshell, Boomers believe success is only achieved through hard work, and there is no replacement for it. You work your way to the top and if you make it, that simply means you are a hard worker and you earned it. If you don't expect to work hard to make it, then you are acting entitled.

There is absolutely nothing wrong with this philosophy. Hard work is a virtue upon which our country was founded. You,

Millennial or Zer, should be prepared to work hard, and I believe you know that. The difference is the way you, verses a Boomer, might define hard work.

The way boomers tend to interpret hard work is with long hours. Visibility is important to them. If they don't see you, they can't know for a fact you're working. I saw this play out many times as a new leader. With the type of role I had, much of my time was spent outside of the office and out in the market stores, with customers or other route salespeople on my team. Although most of my job was outside of the office, my team members still wanted to see me there. I heard them talking many times about managers "not working" because they didn't physically see them present.

Your team, namely your Boomers, will want to see you working, especially at the beginning. It's that simple. As you gain their trust and follow through with your expectations and promises, the need for them to see you all of the time will decrease.

Ways to demonstrate this value:

1. Communicate your schedule- If your team has computers and email, share your calendar or a version of it that lets them know where you are and what you're doing. In the beginning, they will watch it like a hawk. But after they realize they can trust the fact that you are a hard worker dedicated to your team and its success, you'll see your views decrease substantially. Unlike your IG or YouTube videos, this decline in views is a good thing. If your team doesn't

have computers and email, similar to my first team, post a physical copy of your schedule in a location they frequently visit. I used to hang mine outside of my office door or on our team Communication Board.

2. Stay late when possible- Your first year will be a year of learning, anyway. You are naturally going to work more hours in the first year of a role than in any other year, as it will take your longer to do new things and to learn. When you do have to work late, why not stay at the office to do so? This may sound petty but it works. If I was working late and needed to send an email, I would send it to deliver then as opposed to scheduling it to deliver during normal work hours. Why? I wanted my team, namely my skeptical boomers and Xers, to know I was working. Should you do this? Perhaps. As long as you make it clear to your team that you don't expect them to read or respond to late emails, you're good!

3. Be present and work standard hours- Your boss may give you the option to work from home or set your own schedule. If either is the case, make sure you are present as much as possible and work a similar schedule as the majority of your team, especially for the first year. At a minimum, be where your team is at least three, ideally four, days out of the week.

Respect

Although Boomers have a reputation of being somewhat rebellious, they still grew up in a time where respect for your elders was important. Time on earth meant earned respect, in a general sense. This same value translates over to the workplace. **Respect is earned via time invested—***seniority.* This really ties back to their appreciation for hard work and the expectation that those with seniority have earned it by putting in the time and effort.

Whether they are the highest man/woman on the totem pole or the lowest, time—seniority—warrants respect, so they will appreciate receiving that from you.

Despite seniority, however, I've found that Boomers also have a respect for authority/hierarchy in the workplace. I can recall my first team consisting of about 40% Boomers. Frankly, they were never the ones I had trouble with. They weren't super vocal, they didn't often push back and when they did, it was warranted. Perhaps this goes back to their discomfort with conflict. I'm not sure, but they weren't the ones bucking the system. I believe your Boomers will respect your authority—your position—but you'll have to prove to them they should respect *you.*

Ways to demonstrate this value:

1. Celebrate seniority- If you pay attention, you'll notice Boomers wear their seniority within a company like a badge of honor. To you and me, time spent at one company is neither here nor there, but to Boomers and any older generations, it means a lot. Remember their work anniversaries by writing them down or putting them in your calendar. Acknowledge it to them in front of the team, if possible, and give gifts for

the milestone anniversaries—15 years, 20 years, 25 years, etc.—something they can hang on their wall or display in public.

2. Ask for their input (and actually take it)- They've been around longer, so naturally, they know some things you don't. Ask for their opinion sometimes and actually follow through where it makes sense. And give them the credit! I always used to say "Based on your years of experience, what is your take on [insert situation or problem]?"You don't want to do this all of the time, but doing it occasionally shows you respect the time they've put in and the experience they have.

Relationships and the Personal Touch

I always found my Boomer counterparts to be great at sales. They seemed to have the best relationships with their customers and made sales look incredibly easy. They could pick up the phone and move needles it would take me a month of meetings to move. As I watched them over time, I learned they simply had relationships with people. They didn't need to be the most savvy in PowerPoint to build an impressive presentation that wooed a customer. Rather, they relied upon the social capital they'd built over the years and their flat-out knowledge of the business. I noticed the value they put on relationships and how it seemed to make sales easy for them. They understood the value of the personal touch/attention with the customer and I noticed how much it mattered to them.

Generally speaking, Boomers can be relationally-driven and appreciate the personal touch/attention. By reading this chapter, you will see some of the things that matter to them, enabling you to apply that personal touch.

Ways to demonstrate this value:

1. Build unique relationships with each employee- Take the time to build unique relationships with each of the Boomers on your team. What things are they interested in outside of work? Do they have children? Grandchildren? What's in their office or place of business that speaks to who they are? Start a conversation about those things.

2. Apply personal touches to your work- Thank-you notes go a long way. Small tokens of your appreciation, like gift cards or personalized stationery, are often well-received. Look for ways to personalize your gratitude with your team in general, but especially your Boomers.

GEN X

Given that you may have Xer parents, these values may sound very familiar to you. Let's look at how these values might impact the way Xers show up in the workplace.

Balance

I dare say that the number one value for Xers when it comes to work is actually outside of work! It has everything to do with this thing called work/life balance. You'll hear this phrase A LOT as you enter the workplace. Some will argue it is a fallacy that doesn't really exist and you'll find others who believe in it wholeheartedly and are in high pursuit of it. Whether it really exists or not, Xers want it and they are not afraid to voice it and make decisions around it.

As mentioned before, perhaps it has much to do with their latch-key upbringing. I've read before that the average 10 year old Xer spent a whopping 14.5 minutes per day with a significant adult role model. 14.5! Even if that is just directionally correct, I can imagine this wasn't the best experience and that many Xers vowed not to be the same with their kids. They don't want to be like their Traditionalists parents or their Boomer predecessors and be workaholics. They value balance.

Ways to demonstrate this value:

1. Support their defined balance- Ask them what balance means to them in their role, communicate what you will be able to commit to supporting and try your best to do so as much as possible. For example, someone may say, "To me, balance means coaching my daughter's cheerleading team, which requires me to leave work at 4 p.m. on Wednesdays for practice. Is it possible for you to support that?" Then do so. You don't want to show preferential treatment, so maybe ask that they come in an hour earlier on Wednesdays to make up for the time. Have these types of conversations with every member of your team, whether they are Xers or not, and try to support them. I can recall times where I'd go out and work with some of my route salespeople for the

day if they had something important going on for which they needed to get off early. I believe those attempts to align with their definition of balance made deposits into our relational bank accounts that helped me and the team in the long run—when I needed to make withdrawals.

2. Show your own balance- I know, I know. It sounds contradictory, right? Just a few paragraphs ago I told you to make sure your Boomers know you're working hard, and now I'm telling you to show your Xers you have balance. Is that possible? I believe it is. The reason I want you to show your Xers you have balance is to let them know their pursuit of it is okay—that they don't have to work 12 hours a day on your team just to prove that they're working. Which brings me to my last way...

3. Reward performance, not hours- To Xers, speed matters, because speed often means efficiency. They were the first generation to ask *why* to a nine-to-five schedule if the work gets done by two? With Xers, you want to make sure you give them a pat on the back for merits, despite how long it takes. We acknowledge Boomers for their time and performance. We acknowledge Xers for their performance.

Autonomy and Independence

As we've talked about at length, Xers grew up independent and often fending for themselves compared to the generations preceding them. I'd venture to say for this reason, among others, they especially appreciate their independence and freedom in the workplace. They can work in teams, but it's not their preference as it is for Millennials and Boomers. They want to do things their way.

Xers function well when given a task and a little direction to figure it out on their own. Think about it this way—Boomers are about relationships and results in the workplace; Xers are about tasks and results.

Interestingly enough, we see these very tendencies in Xer's children—Gen Z, but we'll save that for later.

Ways to demonstrate this value:

1. Let them be- My mother used to use this phrase a lot. It simply means to leave them alone. Leave them to their own devices and don't force them into group work. Challenge them to collaborate where necessary but don't force them to be collaborative just for the sake of it.

2. Don't micromanage- Give them tasks and let them figure out for themselves whether they need your help or not and when. Micromanaging will stifle a Xer's creativity and productivity. They are at their best when there's freedom to find their own way.

3. Give them as much power as possible- Note that this does not mean give them *all* the power. You are the leader for a reason. However, what I've learned in my 10 years of leading people and businesses is that you will have plenty to be in control of. Where people want power and independence, give it to them until they prove to you they

don't deserve it. When I was a Sales Director, I had about 20 direct reports at any given time. There wasn't enough of me to go around. Believe it or not, I distinctly recall my Xers wanting to see me as little as possible (their territories could be hours away from where my office was located). My Boomers were on the other end of the spectrum, probably because they wanted to build a relationship, ha-ha! I'd give my Xers their autonomy and independence until an issue arose big enough to warrant my attention. I watched many of my peers do the same thing.

Career (over Company)

After seeing their parents get laid off and/or face job insecurity, Gen X has a different perspective on what loyalty is. Instead of remaining blindly loyal to their company as their predecessors and parents did, they're committed to be loyal to their work/career and the people they work with. They work hard, not always to make the company better, but to enhance their careers and the team's performance.

The Gen Xers I've had on my team performed better when they've had clear incentives. They wanted to see the team succeed, but that was often less important to them than their own career development and success. Let us note, there is nothing wrong with this approach to work. It is simply helpful for you to know how to align with team members whose values are structured this way.

Ways to demonstrate this value:

1. Make appeals to them with their career in mind- Asking them to do something because it will be best for the company will not appeal to them. Figure out ways to reframe those requests around the benefits it brings to their careers. For example, let's say the company has a major initiative to improve efficiency in order to cut costs. This Gen X employee at reference has very poor efficiency scores. Sure, we can say, "The company has a huge initiative right now to improve efficiency and yours needs improving. How can we fix it?" Or, to effectively align with this generational value, we could say, "I know you have aspirations to be promoted one day, whether it is here or at another company. Being able to demonstrate you were able to overcome obstacles and improve your efficiency will be a great achievement to highlight your dedication and ability to cut costs. Can we figure out a plan to achieve this?"

2. Provide stretch assignments- As a leader, you're going to have many metrics for which you are responsible—so many that you'll likely need the help of the team to steer the ship in the right direction on each of these metrics. Because Xers are career-driven, providing extra-curricular assignments to them that give them critical experience and the ability to develop some level of differentiating expertise will go a long way. For example, I was ultimately responsible for the Sales, Shrink, Safety, Efficiency, Promotional Execution,

Training, Retention, Accountability and much more for my team. Each year I would appoint Subject Matter Experts to help lead the charge for the team on some of those metrics. This would be an example of a stretch or special assignment.

MILLENNIALS

For many of you, we're about to talk about you—and me, for that matter, so this ought to be fun! Let's take a look at the top three values associated with Millennials in terms of work and how that might impact the way they show up in the workplace. I should preface this by saying some of the values noted for other generations also apply to Millennials, like balance and career over company, and that in an effort to avoid redundancy, I'll introduce different values in my top three.

Meaning/ Sense of Purpose

Boomers want to do meaningful work, as do Xers. The difference between them and Millennials, however, is that the vast majority of Millennials won't settle for **not** doing meaningful work for an extended period of time. They were sold the *you can change the world* dream from their optimistic Boomer parents and apparently it worked, because Millennials believe it is completely possible to do work you love while contributing to the greater good of society. For that reason, they seek out socially responsible companies. Companies who demonstrate care for the environment and companies who take a stand against injustices.

Giving your Millennial team members a clear sense of purpose to their work will be vital to keeping them engaged and getting the most out of them from a performance standpoint.

Ways to demonstrate this value:

1. Make sure they know what the company is doing socially and how they can support it- I remember watching videos of the global food and beverage company I worked for coming to the aid of those impacted by natural disasters like hurricanes, tornados, mudslides, etc. During catastrophic events, it felt good to see the company in which I worked so hard give to those in need. It made me feel like I was doing something to help. I didn't learn about the internal fellowship the company offered until my fifth year with the company. I had to apply for the project, and if I was chosen, I would be able to take a few months away from my job with a team of fellow employees from all over the company and together we lend our business skills to help local communities address societal challenges. Making sure your Millennials know about opportunities like these in your company will help you engage them as a leader. If your company matches charitable donations made by employees, make sure they know that, too.

2. Communicate in terms of impact- For Gen X, we talked about making appeal with career in mind. This applies to Millennials, as well, but they are not concerned only about their careers. Some would argue they're even more

concerned with making an impact. For that reason, make appeals to them within the context of the impact their work will make.

3. Give them time to volunteer- Maybe your company gives a certain amount of paid time for employees to volunteer every year. If not, perhaps your leaders would be open to starting that based on your recommendation. Giving Millennials time to support the causes for which they're passionate matters.

Personal Attention

Maybe it has something to do with the helicopter parents they had growing up, but Millennials like personal attention, just as their Boomer parents do. They want as much feedback as possible and place a high value on mentorship/ coaching. They have high goals and expect their bosses and managers to assist and mentor them in attaining those goals.

As a young Millennial leader, I don't know if it's feedback I wanted so much as assurance and guidance. Having never led people before, I knew I just wanted to make sure I was doing things the right way. Which is really why I wrote this book—to serve as a source of guidance for people in the position I was once in. Sure, your managers and mentors will be able to help your through some of this stuff, but you don't always want to ask them for help or attention, ha-ha.

Ways to demonstrate this value:

1. Establish a regular cadence to feedback- With Millennials, I recommend establishing a regular schedule for feedback up front and more importantly, sticking to it. Depending on the level of my team, I held weekly one-on-one meetings with each of my team members. My Xers didn't mind at all when we needed to cancel for one reason or other. My Millennials…not so much.

2. Spend individual time at least two-to-four times a year- Try to work with all of your team members one-on-one at least once a year. This time should be spent coaching, learning and spending quality time with them. Some people will dread this time with you, or at least act like they do, and others—your Millennials—will love it. Out of all the things you have to do, you're taking a good part of a day to spend with them personally. Since I became a leader at F&B, my goal was to work with every person on my team quarterly, and at the minimum, twice a year. For me, those were some of my best days, and my goal was to make it the same way for my team. It meant a lot to them, especially my younger leaders…and Boomers, too.

Achievement

You'll hear people say things about Millennials being entitled when it comes to many things, promotions in the workplace included. While that may be true in some cases, I truly believe that the

Millennial's desire for rapid advancement in the workplace has less do with entitlement and more to do with the value they've put on achievement ever since childhood.

In grade school, many Millennials grew up with high performance standards hanging over their heads, either by parents, the school system or their peers. Their Baby Boomer parents were far more educated than previous generations were and consequently, Millennials were constantly tested and compared to other students. This conditioned them to perform and be rewarded for the performance. They are ambitious, motivated by the opportunity for advancement and are used to seeing immediate results. (Think about what they've experienced with technological trends like gaming and the Internet...immediate feedback and instantaneous results.)

For your Millennial team members, it will be important to reward their performance and acknowledge their achievements. The best way to acknowledge someone's achievement in the workplace is to acknowledge they can do more—*promotions*!

Ways to demonstrate this value:

1. Track and highlight performance- During my time at F&B Company, I tracked performance weekly on several key metrics. On my team's communication board, I posted results from the prior week and highlighted top performance. I then did a monthly roll up and a quarterly roll up. Highlighting performance in this way is important,

but it is just as important, if not more important, to ensure you reward that performance.

2. Talk about what it takes for promotion- I'm about to make this really simple for you. Ready? Okay...GIFT THEM A COPY OF THIS BOOK! This book will tell them the unwritten things they need to do to be considered for promotion, that you may not be able to verbally communicate to them.

GEN Z

We are about to talk about most of you! Yes you...Gen Z! Let's take a look at the top three values associated with Gen Z in terms of work and how that may impact the way they show up in the workplace. There are only a couple of waves of Centennials in the corporate workplace, so our knowledge of them is not as robust as it is for the other generations, but we can make inferences based on what we do know (from their time in school and life thus far). Like prior generations we've discussed, some of the above values apply, like meaning and independence, but in an effort to avoid redundancy, I'll introduce different values in my top three.

Financial Security

Gen Z watched their Xer parents go through the largest economic downturn in the Americas since the Great Depression. They saw their parents get laid off, lose their savings to the stock market, see their homes foreclosed on and more. Observing this, coupled with watching their Millennial predecessors suffer from mounds of student loan debt, has a given Gen Z higher focus on financial security.

A study conducted by Adecco found that Gen Z's top career aspiration is financial stability. 31% of those surveyed said they prefer stability, while only 28% said they prefer to work their dream job.[1] 56% of high school students discussed saving money with their parents in the last 6 months.[2]

Ways to demonstrate this value:

1. Understand compensation and benefits- Be able to explain compensation packages, read pay stubs and explain different types of benefits. Because they seek financial security, they will be inquisitive, but they will also fact check against the Internet. Being able to accurately explain your level of expertise will be important in gaining credibility and trust in the eyes of your Gen Z team members.

2. Provide education around compensation, benefits and finances- My organization recently piloted a conference for interns in the Charlotte area. We thought the conversation around personal finance management was important, so we provided optional after-hours panel discussions around the subject with some fintech leaders in the Charlotte business community. We received great feedback around the session, but the interns actually suggested it should have been a mandatory session during our day conference. This speaks to the value these Gen Z interns put on financial literacy.

Maybe consider having your finance support person do a five-minute segment in your monthly meeting or draw up a one pager that covers one topic per month.

Inclusion

Gen Z is the most ethnically diverse generation on the planet to date. They grew up in classrooms with peers of all different cultural backgrounds and find diversity and inclusion to be quite normal and natural. Think about it...they don't know a time where the President of the United States wasn't a black man. For this reason, they expect a company to be inclusive, and if it isn't, it's a sign they can't be trusted. In a study done by Ernst and Young, Gen Z reported that the number one factor in trusting an employer is equality.[3] Six-out-of-ten said they will support a brand if that company stands for equal rights in sexual orientation and race.

The bottom line is inclusion is not optional for Gen Z. Making sure your team culture is inclusive will help retain this vivacious generation emerging in the workplace.

Ways to demonstrate this value:

1. Establish an inclusive team culture from Day One- Welcome the opinions of all and actually execute suggestions made by all types of team members—of different races, ages, sexual orientations, religions, disability, etc. Diversity is making sure everyone has a voice. Inclusion is making sure each voice is heard.

2. Hire diverse candidates- If you play a role in the hiring of your team members, do all you can possibly do to ensure you have a diverse talent pool and are hiring based on qualifications and not biased classifications like how well they'd fit in with your current team. Look for additions to your team that will bring different perspectives by way of their experiences.

Freedom/Autonomy

Similar to their Xer parents, Gen Z is drawn to autonomy. If the world thought Millennials were multitaskers, Centennials must be omni-taskers! They've grown up with a television in the background, a laptop on their lap, an iPad on the couch and a cell phone in their right hand. Multitasking is pretty much how they've always lived. The same can be said when it comes to their work lives. They want the security of a standard nine-to-five but they are also very entrepreneurial, which introduces the side hustle!

Building websites, driving for Uber, running the social media account for the local pizzeria, freelancing on Upwork or hosting an Airbnb—all of these are different types of side hustles your Gen Zers are probably doing, either themselves, or else they know friends who do. How you welcome their entrepreneurial spirits and respect their desire for autonomy will make a difference in how they contribute to your team and for how long.

Ways to demonstrate this value:

1. Give them space for their creativity- Being technologically advanced and entrepreneurial lends to a certain level of creativity. Give your Gen Z members space to apply their creativity and flex their entrepreneurial muscles. I am a businesswoman first, but I also have a very creative side. I believe I can thank my father for these things. Running my first district at F&B Company was awesome, but I'd often come home to my makeshift home studio and write songs to express myself creatively. Keeping the two separately didn't last for long because I am one being. Over time I began to see opportunities for me to apply my creative side in the business world. I designed a t-shirt for our annual Susan G. Komen race participation, fancy invitations for the retirement festivities of some of our vets, and later in my career, produced a motivational video that would spread across the country. Rather than be intimidated by your Zers' entrepreneurial spirits, give them space to let that spirit wander for the betterment of the company, your team and their careers.

2. Talk about side hustles- We know many Gen Zers will have side hustles and if we're honest, these days, many other generations do, too. If your company has clear rules about these, especially where there could be a conflict of interest, ensure people know where the red tape is. If you have a side hustle, maybe discussing that in a one-on-one conversation

with your Zer would be a good way to build rapport. I'm simply saying—we all have them. If they are appropriate, why hide them?

———～～———

I know that was a lot of information. Do you have to demonstrate every one of those values in every way? No. It'd be really hard for you to do that, especially being new to your role. As we've discussed a lot now, this book is a guide; a resource for which to refer back when needed. Once you get the makeup of your team, focus on demonstrating one value with one group for one month. See how it goes. Do the same for another group the next month, and so on.

Another way to think about leveraging what you've just learned is to consider having core values for your team. Perhaps some of these values, depending on the generational makeup of your team, are already incorporated. This will be a major part of your team's identity. Or consider embedding some of these in your individual leadership philosophy, which we'll talk more about in Rule #5.

RULE #3: COMMUNICATE THEIR WAY

#communication

#empathy

#collaboration

As a mid-level leader, communication will be first and foremost. Generally speaking, the vision is set, the mission is articulated, the goals are derived, and the objectives are made clear by someone many levels above you. Your primary job is to figure out how to best communicate those goals and priorities to mobilize your team towards an execution that achieves said results. I know I just made your job sound way easier than it actually is, but it's true. You are there to communicate what's already been determined and to then get it done. Your ability to get it done, though, is directly correlated to your ability to communicate. Leadership cannot be effective without effective communication. Communication is a core leadership competency.

As a leader, the more people, you have to communicate with, accompanied by their own unique experiences and perspectives, the more complex the task becomes. Why? Because people communicate in different ways. Men communicate differently than women. Teens communicate differently than adults. People from the south communicate differently than people from the north. And the list goes on. Trying to communicate one message in one way to a team of more than one person requires consideration, empathy and some context.

For that reason, I've dedicated an entire chapter and rule to understanding the differences in communication preferences across the active generations in the workplace. You will eventually get to know the individual communication styles of each person on your team, but going into your role with a little context on at least one generation descriptor can be helpful.

Let's start by looking at the evolution of communication over time.

Figure 4.1[1]

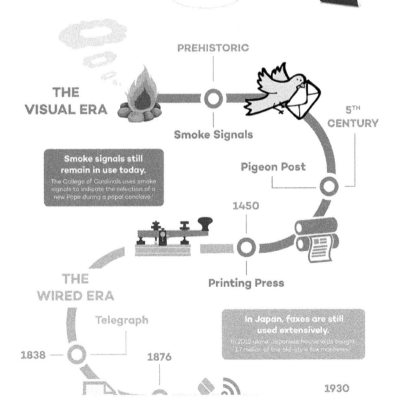

A HISTORY OF
COMMUNICATION

Throughout the ages, humankind has developed various modes of communication to connect, engage, and interact with one another. As technology has evolved, so have the opportunities to communicate more rapidly and productively.

Here is a look at the evolution of communication.

PREHISTORIC

THE VISUAL ERA

Smoke Signals

5TH CENTURY

Smoke signals still remain in use today.
The College of Cardinals uses smoke signals to indicate the selection of a new Pope during a papal conclave.

Pigeon Post

1450

THE WIRED ERA

Printing Press

Telegraph

In Japan, faxes are still used extensively.
In 2012 alone, Japanese households bought 1.7 million of the old-style fax machines.

1838

1876

1930

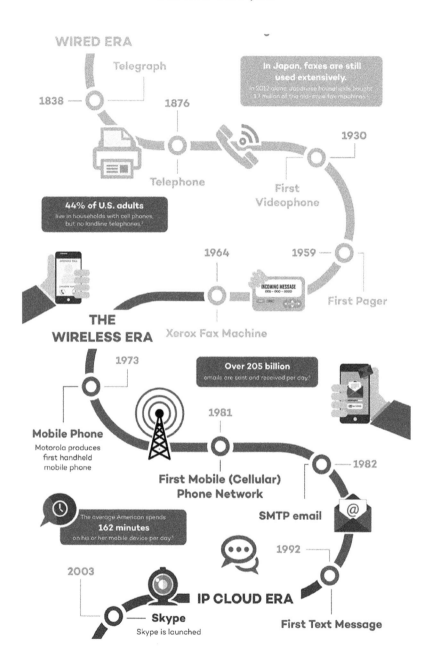

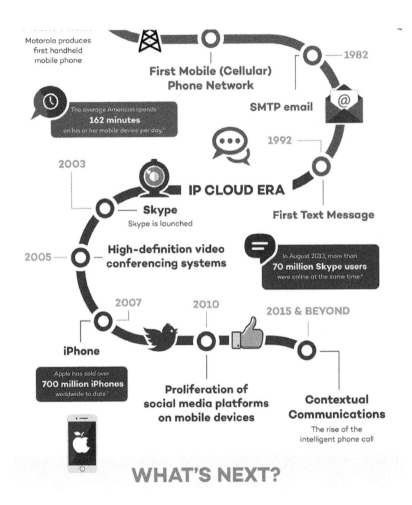

Motorola produces first handheld mobile phone

First Mobile (Cellular) Phone Network

1982

The average American spends **162 minutes** on his or her mobile device per day.

SMTP email

1992

IP CLOUD ERA

2003

Skype
Skype is launched

First Text Message

High-definition video conferencing systems

2005

In August 2013, more than **70 million Skype users** were online at the same time.

2007

2010

2015 & BEYOND

iPhone

Apple has sold over **700 million iPhones** worldwide to date.

Proliferation of social media platforms on mobile devices

Contextual Communications
The rise of the intelligent phone call

WHAT'S NEXT?

Let's take a look at the communication preferences of each generation in the workplace and make some attempt to understand why they relate the way they do.

BABY BOOMERS

Do you remember the telephone example I gave in *Chapter 1: Understanding the Generations* when discussing the speed at which technology moves in today's world? In that example, you may recall my mentioning Baby Boomers growing up in a world free of cell phones, spottily-littered with fax machines and these small devices called pagers. A pager, also known as a beeper, is a wireless device that displays alphanumeric messages and sometimes voice messages, depending on the type of pager you had. One-way pagers came first, which allowed a person to send a numeric message from a landline phone to the recipient's pager. The message would display something like **704-555-1424** or **143** (which meant *I love you*). The recipient would receive a beep or a buzz to their pager and would, hopefully, follow the instructions. If those instructions included making a call, they would have to locate a landline telephone on which to make that call. Two-way pagers came later, which allowed them to acknowledge, reply to and originate alphanumeric messages using the pager. An example would be, **Call your mother now**. Two-way pagers could not send calls, only texts, but could still be "called" like the one-way pagers I mentioned above. This is about as close as people could get to text messaging at that time. Text messaging as we know it today didn't come about until 1992, when Boomers were between the ages of 28ish and 46ish.

Perhaps this helps you understand why your grandparents and maybe even your parents aren't the best texters and sometimes shy away from it. Some of them were 25 years into their professional careers before the first text message was even sent! Consider that same fact when communicating with your Boomer team members.

It may be easier for you to communicate by way of text message, but know that it is likely not that way for them. Boomers grew up in a time where the average conversation, much less a business conversation, was done either via phone or in a face-to-face conversation. For this reason, you may notice their default mode of communication will often be phone or face-to-face. When you text them, they may actually call you back! If they do text back, it will likely be short, sweet and to the point. After all, character limits on pagers were indeed a real thing.

While you may find it absolutely normal, Boomers may find doing business via text message unprofessional. As I think back to my time leading teams, the best communication happened face-to-face. When we weren't in the same vicinity, phone calls were a solid second option. Despite my initial discomfort with both, I had to quickly get over it if I wanted to be the leader they needed.

Their workaholic work ethic, coupled with their relationally-driven value structure in the workplace, creates this *call anytime* attitude from your Boomers. It will be important for you establish your expectations around communication up front. What are the team's do-not-disturb hours? We'll cover this more in Rule #5.

GEN X

Unlike Baby Boomers, Gen X is very well acquainted with cell phones. Many Xers weren't even born when the first cell phone was put to use, so they've truly seen and experienced the evolution of cell phones. They are much more tech savvy than their Boomer predecessors and navigate cell phones with the best of us Millennials. (I don't think they have anything on you Zers, though!) To them, texting is a viable option, but they prefer email as their number one business communication tool.

Like Facetime is for Millennials, email is the hot new groundbreaking communication tool of Gen X's time. It completely changed the course of business and just so happened to have done so right when many Xers were entering their careers. The Xers to arrive years later wouldn't know a time in business where email wasn't a thing. You and I, Millennial/Centennial, certainly don't. With that said, you'll likely find in communicating with your team that your Xers steer more toward email than texts or even phone and face-to-face communication. While they are far more comfortable with the latter two than Millennials and Centennials, in their desire for efficiency and, some believe, air cover, email seems to be their option of choice.

I recall speaking with a Centennial client of mine recently and her complaining about how she'll text her mother with a very quick and simple question and her mother will actually email her back! I thought this was hilarious, but as I began to think about my time leading Xers, I'm reminded of how lengthy and frequent their email communications used to be. Sometimes I'd actually pick up the phone and call in response to an email to save myself the time writing back!

When communicating with your Gen X team members, know that they'll likely err toward email. As inconvenient as it may be for you, emailing them may make them feel more comfortable.

MILLENNIALS

Millennials grew up with AOL Instant Messenger, character limit text messaging, chat rooms and some of the first forms of social media on the Internet like Myspace, and Friendster. They're used to fast, convenient communication in their personal lives and want the same thing in the workplace. Text messaging and Instant Messenger therefore takes the lead as their default communication preferences. Email is a close second, but it probably comes as no surprise to anyone that their last communication choice is talking on the phone. Many credit this to the amount of time spent behind screens—cell phones and computers alike. Regardless of the exact reason, the average millennial will pass on a phone conversation versus a text or an email—and don't even think about leaving a voicemail! There are probably about 20 unopened voicemails in my cell phone mailbox right now.

As a Millennial leader, appeasing your Millennial team members on this preferred method of communication probably won't be very hard. However, I urge you to consider it as one of your jobs as a leader to develop your team members, helping them close some of their capability gaps to become better professionals, more prepared for the next level. While your Millennial team members may default to texting versus verbally having difficult conversations, that won't suffice as they advances in their careers. You'll need to challenge them to become comfortable where they are uncomfortable.

GEN Z

Recent surveys show that contrary to popular belief, Gen Z actually prefers face-to-face, in-person communication over IM or email.[2] Some believe they are more comfortable with face-to-face time than Millennials because of the prevalence of Facetime and other video-conferencing apps. The average Gen Zer won't remember a time where they weren't able to see the person to whom they were talking on a screen if they so choose.

Another reason some believe Gen Z prefers face-to-face communication is because they have witnessed the bad wrap Millennials have gotten for not being able to have face-to-face conversations. They are aware of the impact copious amounts of screen time has on their communication skills and they know they'll have to be intentional about working that muscle until it's strong. In a study conducted by the Center for Generational Kinetics, 45% of Gen Z said they wish they had stronger communication skills.[3]

As a leader, it will be important that you aide your Gen Zers in developing the communication skills they so desire. Communicate their way and teach them how to communicate others' ways. I believe their biggest challenge coming into your team from a communication standpoint will be email. For that reason, I've included an entire rule about it in Rule #21 to help guide them and you.

PUTTING IT ALL TOGETHER

In my first leadership role at F&B Company, we had boatloads of communications tools. Because my team spent 98% of their days in the field, outside of the F&B office and inside the stores servicing our customers, using these tools was vital to disperse information because there was no shouting over the cubicle wall. We had a voicemail system, handheld messages, personal cell phones (for calls or text messages), team communications boards and individual mailboxes. We also had weekly one-on-one, in-person meetings. Said differently, there were seven different ways a team member could receive communication from their leader. *Seven*! Talk about overwhelming and inefficient. If I had no structure, my team would spend 30 minutes a day checking these options for possible information needed to do their jobs. Way too much. At that time there was no Dropbox or Google Docs, so add those in today and there are even more options! (You're probably wondering where the email is. They didn't have email addresses because there was no way for them to check email in the field. The handhelds were too old.)

As a leader, it was my responsibility to create a communication plan that worked for my team. I needed to determine which, out of all seven options, which ones best fit the makeup of my team and why. So what did I do? I tried using them all, because they all existed for a reason, right? Mistake Number One. After that proved to be ineffective, I chose what I thought would be best for the team based on (a) what made the most sense and (b) what would be easiest and most efficient for me. Mistake Number Two. When that proved to be ineffective, I decided to do what I'm advising you to do from Day One—I asked my team in our monthly district meeting which would be best for them. Some said text (mainly my Xers and Millennials), others said notes in their mailbox or a phone call (my Boomers). There were some differences, but the consensus was handheld messages were ineffective and the voicemail system required too much work. Those two came off the board. Our weekly meetings were a company mandate, so those weren't going anywhere, and our communications board was helpful when needed. So we agreed that for one-off, time-sensitive communications, I would call those who preferred calls and text those who preferred texts. If it involved more than three team members, I would text regardless of their preference. We'd use the mailboxes for important printed information not requiring immediate action and include general information on the communications board that people could grab or snap picture of as needed (I also used that board to highlight performance).

Lastly, we determined our communications hours. Honest moment. Many in my team began their routes around 5 a.m. On office days, I'm not in the office until about 7:30 a.m. The last thing I wanted was a call at 5 a.m. about something that could have waited until eight! On the opposite side, I often worked until 6:30 p.m. and sometimes later. Some of my route salesmen were done at 3:00 p.m. and the last thing they wanted was a call from me at 6:30 p.m. about something that could have waited until the following morning. So, we established *do-not-disturb* hours except for emergency cases. We then spent time aligning on what constituted an emergency.

The result? We finally got into a rhythm when it came to communication, our execution improved and frustration decreased. Were there times we needed to go off of this plan for special reasons? Absolutely. But the power was in the fact that generally speaking, my team knew what to expect from me in terms of communication and vice-versa. Based on their preferences, I was able to tailor our communication plan to accommodate the team.

As you prepare to lead your multigenerational team, I'd give the following advice to ensure you **communicate their way**:

- Seek their feedback- Before you establish a communication plan, seek the team's opinion on what has or hasn't worked in the past and what they suggest going forward.

- Establish expectations up-front and together- Establish do not disturb hours. How do you handle emergencies? What constitutes as an emergency?

- Attempt to strike a balance between the different modes of communication in your final communication plan- Use a combination of modes like text, email, phone, in-person and instant messaging, file sharing, etc. In what situations do we text versus email? In what situations do we call? We touch on this a little later in Rule #21.

- Be as efficient as possible, but understand this approach may require some redundancy- You may have to call your two Boomer to discuss the group text you just sent to the entire team. That's okay.

PART TWO:

ON THE JOB

Rules for Leading
Your Multigenerational Team

RULE #4: KNOW U DK

#humility
#selfawareness
#selfassessment

You're about to start your new job and you are PUMPED. (I'm super pumped for you, by the way.) You've done your research on the company and have read the first few chapters of this book—which means you understand the difference in value systems and communication preferences across generations. You're already on the right track!

So what's the next thing you need to do before heading into the office, otherwise known as the generational war zone? It starts with a simple affirmation that some will likely not see as that. Take a deep breath, look yourself in the mirror, and say verbatim:

> *You don't know everything, you don't have to know everything and you're not expected to know everything.*

It may seem like a simple, mundane task right now, but I promise you this is effective for several reasons: First, it helps relieve some of the self-imposed pressure you've likely taken on as a soon-to-be leader in the *real world*. It's easy to think because you are the newbie, you have to prove yourself by knowing everything, or at least pretending to.

Secondly, it reminds you of what the average person expects from you as a new employee to the organization or to the position. As a soon-to-be leader of people who are in many cases older than you, you're going to want to believe you were hired because of what you know today, and therefore feel the need to demonstrate that wealth of knowledge. This is as untrue as the sky is purple. You were not hired because of what you know today; you were hired because of what you stand to know tomorrow. In other words, you were hired because of your potential. And everyone knows that. No one expects you to come on board knowing everything. It's unrealistic in general terms but even more so for millennials and Gen Zers in leadership training programs.

Lastly, it helps position your mind and spirit in a place of humility. The best learning occurs from a place of humility. Mentally and spiritually positioning yourself to receive knowledge and wisdom from anyone is key to your rapid growth and maturation in your new role. Saying this affirmation daily centers you and brings you back into this place to receive.

Let's practice again.

> *You don't know everything, you don't
> have to know everything and you're not
> expected to know everything.*

Once you've affirmed you're in a space of learning to yourself, it is time to let others know. And yes, you'll have to do it verbally, as uncomfortable as it might be. But this also involves some important non-verbal communication as well, which we'll cover.

Let's imagine your first formal introduction to your team. In the next chapter, we'll thoroughly cover how to properly make this introduction, but for now we'll jump ahead to help you tackle a specific part of your initial introduction that directly relates to this chapter. At some point during your first interaction with your **entire** team, it is vital that **you acknowledge to them that you don't know everything**. They, of course, already know this, but you acknowledging it exemplifies one key characteristic of all great leaders—humility. We've mentioned that word a lot in this chapter, right? That's because it's so important to effective leadership in general, but even more so for new leaders.

If you're like me, you are probably worried about looking weak to your new subordinates, something you see as being detrimental to your brand. You're thinking, *I'm already young...I want my team to see strength when they look at me, not weakness.* Allow me to reassure you—making this admission to your team doesn't make you look weak. It makes you look **teachable**. No one wants to be led by a know-it-all, especially an inexperienced 20-something know-it-all. To appear teachable is to appear human. And believe it or not, you are human and you don't have the superpowers you've always dreamed about. However, to be humble and teachable is a power indeed. It comes from a place of strength, perhaps contrary to your initial belief of seeing it as being weak.

When you communicate this admission to your team, you do not have to sound defeated or *woe is me*. You are not looking for pity; you are simply acknowledging a fact and making a quick deposit into the Bank of Emotional Intelligence by showing a moment of vulnerability. But you don't have to LOOK vulnerable. Be **confidently humble**. And yes, there is absolutely a such thing!

To be confidently humble is to be so comfortable in a place of humility that you actually exude confidence. You are extremely comfortable with the fact that you don't know everything today because you know—from our handy affirmation—that you don't *have to* and you are not *expected to*. The confidence in this situation is actually a two-fold work of beauty. You are confident in yourself that you can, and will, learn everything. And you are confident that your team knows enough to keep things afloat while you learn and is smart enough to teach you quite a bit. Acknowledging the confidence you have in them and yourself during your first formal introduction is optional, but a great idea.

Let's look at a few examples of how you can admit to your team that you don't know everything in a confidently humble way.

> **Preface: "I'm so excited to have the honor of leading this phenomenal team to what I believe will be even greater heights than you have already reached….**

Example A: I have a ton to learn as I get rooted in the organization, but I'm eager to listen and learn from everyone, especially you."

Example B: You guys are so knowledgeable. I'm just here to learn and take our execution of that knowledge to the next level."

Example C: I don't have all the answers, but I plan to ask the right questions until I get the answers we all need to be successful. Many of those questions will be posed to you."

Example D: I know I have a lot to learn and I'm eager to do so."

All of these statements display humility and demonstrate confidence at that same time.

Now that you are able to verbally communicate you don't know it all, let's talk about the non-verbal indicators you can use to communicate the same, thus reinforcing what we have verbally shared. After all, what you say is important, but even more important is how you act. When verbal and non-verbal communication are incongruent, people will believe the non-verbal. For this reason, non-verbally communicating you don't know everything is just as important, if not more important, than verbally communicating it.

One way to communicate humility and an openness to learn from your team is by sitting next to them versus across from them in one-on-one meetings. This small gesture makes the team member more comfortable and facilitates a feeling of partnership versus subordination.

Another way to communicate openness to learn from your team is through delegation, particularly in a public setting. For instance, you notice morale is low amongst the team and decide to incorporate a Camaraderie Captain role to help solve the problem. You notice one of your team members is particularly influential amongst the team and good at making people feel good. You assign this person the Camaraderie Captain role and give them 10 minutes in every team meeting to discuss his/her ideas to boost rapport, engage the team in the implementation process and report results.

There are many benefits to delegating responsibility to solve *large* problems to your team and an increased feeling of partnership is one of them. It demonstrates your trust in your team and also speaks to your humility as a leader, which is exactly what you are trying to accomplish. You are not on a power trip and you don't need the glory of solving every problem. You know your team members are better suited to influence certain areas of the business and you are confidently humble enough to allow them to do it. Also, be sure to give them the credit—in front of their peers, your peers, and your leadership. It may sound like it won't make you look good—but trust me, it will. The best leaders are able to get things done through others.

The last way we will discuss to non-verbally communicate openness to learning from your team is simply to work with them. Pick a day at random and just show up. Depending on their job, sit with them, work alongside them, and listen. Your intention is not to lead on this day—it's to listen and help. If you are a manager at Target and you work with one of your stockers for a day, simply help them stock. If a case of soda bursts open all over your crisply dry-cleaned red button-down shirt, rub it in and keep throwing cases! Why, you might ask? It's not like you don't have anything better to do, right? It shows your team member that you are not above the work they do. You are willing to get your hands dirty and get into the weeds of the business. You are not only interested in learning about the daily obstacles of their job, but you want to experience them. You are interested in hearing and seeing the business from their vantage points.

Now, the key to this having a lasting impact is that you actually go back and work to remove one or two of the obstacles they mentioned to you or that you observed. You'll see and hear a lot, but fixing one or two issues will go a long way in building trust and establishing the rapport you desire with your team.

The benefits of communicating and demonstrating humility are endless. It builds trust, makes you look good, establishes rapport, empowers your team members, evokes change, drive results and so much more. Admitting you don't know everything demonstrates humility early and sets the stage for such things to occur.

Remember your affirmation and say it to yourself daily for the first three-to-four months in your new role.

> *I don't know everything, I don't have to know everything and I'm not expected to know everything.*

As our boy Kendrick Lamar put it so eloquently—*Be humble. Sit down.*

RULE #5: GIVE A PROPER INTRODUCTION

#publicspeaking
#presentationskills
#verbalcommunication
#visualcommunication
#organization
#meetingmanagement

Research shows it takes seven seconds to make a first impression. You have seven seconds to be hated or loved. Respected or disregarded. Mature or immature. Real or fake. Talk about pressure!

By the time you get the first opportunity to formally introduce yourself to your entire team, you may have already had very short interactions with them individually or they may know of you from seeing or hearing of you during your training or onboarding phases. Those interactions are important and certainly contribute to the first impression left on the minds of your team members, but the formal group introduction carries the most weight. For this reason,

I am going to walk you through how to make a proper formal introduction to your team, one that will lead to respect and being taken seriously.

First let's talk about the goal of your first formal introduction. As a leader, young or old, your ultimate goal in your initial interaction with your team is to build rapport and gain trust/respect. It is not to be liked. Hopefully that comes as an added bonus, but it should not be your primary goal. Many young leaders make the mistake of focusing on being liked by their team rather than being respected. They want to be the cool boss rather than the effective boss. The hope is *if I'm cool and they like me, then I'll be effective.* In order to be a successful leader, you'll need to switch that ideology around, and it's best you do it sooner rather than later. **If you are effective, then you are cool.**

In order to be effective early on, you'll need to build rapport that leads to understanding the needs of your team, and gain their trust and respect by demonstrating the capability of meeting those needs. If you effectively build rapport, the like will follow. It may not follow immediately, but it will come. Trust me. It's what I call deferred appreciation, which we will talk more about in a later chapter.

Now that we have clearly established our goal is to build rapport and gain trust and respect, let's cover the step-by-step process to building an introduction presentation which does just that. Sometimes your training division will provide a template for you, but in the case they don't, I've got you covered. Just head over to my website (www.ravensolomon.com), visit the **Leading Your Parents** tab and download a template I've built just for you from the Resources section!

BUILDING A PROPER INTRODUCTION

Step 1: Prepare

There are two things you are going to want to prepare before you formally introduce yourself to your new team—your presentation and the meeting space. Throughout the remainder of the process we'll cover how to build the presentation.

Making this introduction should not be taken lightly. It's your seven-second first impression, remember? You only get one opportunity to make a first impression, so you really want to invest the time to prepare for this. With that being said, set aside 30 minutes the morning of or the evening before your presentation to set up your meeting space. Make sure the projector works, the clicker has batteries, your computer hooks up properly, the tables are arranged how you would like and so on. You don't want to be scrambling trying to get the space ready 10 minutes before your meeting is scheduled to start. If you're anything like me, that will throw you off mentally and disrupt your intended flow. This is a big deal. Take the necessary time to make sure things run well beforehand. To reiterate, this should be done 8-24 hours before your presentation, if possible, so you have time to react just in case something goes wrong.

For example, let's say the projector was broken two days ago but no one mentioned it to you. You get there to set up your meeting space only to realize your entire team will be huddled up looking at your 15.5 inch laptop screen if you don't make something happen quick! If this is discovered the evening before your meeting, you have the morning to stroll into Best Buy, purchase an ungodly expensive projector (who knew!?) in plenty of time to get it set up and running for your meeting. (We'll talk about company credit cards at another time! ☺) On the other hand, if you've waited to set up until 10 minutes before your meeting was scheduled to start, your team will be getting to know one another far more intimately than they would probably like!

It is important to note also that being prepared sends the right message to your team—you value and respect their time.

Note: Greet each team member personally before the meeting starts. Don't spend time in the meeting making them go around and introduce themselves because that will only be for you. (Unless of course there are new team members and/or other personnel changes have occurred). Chances are they know each other already.

Step 2: Start Personal

The first step in building rapport is to find common ground in order to relate. You want to humanize yourself with the intention of relating to your team members as a human being, not just their boss. You want to give them a glimpse into who you are as a person. Where are you from? What is your favorite pastime? Favorite football team? Favorite band? Fun fact? three words that best describe you? Who does your immediate family comprise of? What is most important to you? All of these are example questions to get you to think about what lighthearted yet introspective things you might share with your team to build rapport.

Do *not* share your age! Sure, they may be able to figure it out, but there is no need to outright disclose your age. No 55-year-old leader is doing that, right? You shouldn't either. If you are asked, though you shouldn't be, there is no need to lie. You can either share or politely decline, by saying something to the effect of, *"Ya know, I try not to discuss that at work,"* or *"Honestly, I'd rather not share,"* or for women, *"A lady never tells her age."* But you certainly don't want to voluntarily disclose your age. Your age has nothing to do with your capabilities, and that fact applies to any age.

Try to keep it to family, professional experiences, life-shaping experiences, personality traits, personal values, sports, music and other hobbies. Consider your audience. Remember the goal is to find common ground.

Step 3: Your Professional Background

Unless your professional background is super extensive and includes lots of experience which directly correlates to you being an effective leader of the team to whom you are speaking, you should not spend a significant amount of time on this section. Think of it like an abbreviated resume. You only put pertinent information on your resume and you do it in a clean and concise fashion. Make this no more than 50% of your resume.

You'll want to cover the school you attended, what your degree is in, perhaps why you chose that field of study and any relevant experience that either demonstrates your *depth as a person* or *your capability as a leader or a professional.* If the experience doesn't speak to one or both of those it is not relevant. In other words, no one cares what sorority or fraternity you were in. I know you may be highly offended by that if you are a part of one but it's true. Those are no more than Greek letters with which your team likely has no connection. However, if you led community service efforts for your fraternity or sorority and the experience helped shape your beliefs on being a servant leader, that is worth mentioning. Make sense?

Another example might be your job(s) while in college. Your three years spent dropping fries at Chick-fil-A really doesn't matter. However, if through that you learned the importance of hard work, worked your way to car ownership or climbed the ladder to Assistant Manager, that speaks to your capabilities as a leader and professional. It shows you are willing to put in the work, are diligent and have been previously identified for your leadership abilities, albeit in a completely different ballgame.

Another tip—save the acronyms. The average person doesn't know what NSBE is. If the organization fits the qualifications for sharing listed above, use the full name and be sure to verbally explain what the organization is or does. This is especially important if you are leading a team of technical or frontline employees who may not have gone to a university. Again, I say, remember your audience. At this point in your career, you're used to communicating within a community who speaks relatively the same language. It might be challenging to mentally adjust from that level of communicative comfort, but you can do it. Be intentional.

Step 4: Explain Your Leadership Philosophy and Style

You may not know much about your leadership style at this point, but you do have thoughts on what you think leadership is. That is your leadership philosophy. We will use that philosophy to quickly identify a foundational leadership style for you. I say *foundational* because your leadership style, and maybe even your philosophy, will mold and shape itself over time. You will learn more and more about yourself and your interactions with the world—and people—will evolve. As you grow personally and professionally and experience more, the way you lead will grow, as well.

The second thing to note as we consider your leadership style is that the best, most experienced leaders adjust their leadership style by situation. Some team members require one leadership style while others require another. One project may call for a hands-on approach, while most day-to-day work permits a hands-off approach. This is called **situational leadership®** and it is a valuable and necessary skill to development. However, regardless of our ability to adapt our leadership styles based on the situation, we all have a default leadership style from which we tend to operate. What we are trying to convey to your team is just that. In what way are you most comfortable leading? Note: Your default can be a blend of two styles.

There are tons of leadership styles out there. I mean TONS. I will offer six, explain some key characteristics of each style and allow you to choose. When sharing your style with your team, it's important to note that you don't have to use the leadership style title or the description I've selected. They are mainly interested in hearing the characteristics.

To recap:

> **Leadership Philosophy**- What you believe leadership means and why

> **Leadership Style**- How you personally tend to lead (in most scenarios)

Leadership Styles

I love Daniel Goleman's assessment of the six different leadership styles most prevalent in the workplace. There are certainly other assessments out there, but I like the simplicity of his.

Chart 5.1[1]

	Commanding	Visionary	Affiliative	Democratic	Pacesetting	Coaching
The leader's modus operandi	Demands immediate compliance	Mobilizes people toward a vision	Creates harmony and builds emotional bonds	Forges consensus through participation	Sets high standards for performance	Develops people for the future
The style in a phrase	"Do what I tell you."	"Come with me."	"People come first."	"What do you think?"	"Do as I do, now."	"Try this."
Underlying emotional intelligence competencies	Drive to achieve, initiative, self-control	Self-confidence, empathy, change catalyst	Empathy, building relationships, communication	Collaboration, team leadership, communication	Conscientiousness, drive to achieve, initiative	Developing others, empathy, self-awareness
When the style works best	In a crisis, to kickstart a turnaround, or with problem employees	When changes require a new vision, or when a clear direction is needed	To heal rifts in a team or to motivate people during stressful circumstances	To build buy-in or consensus, or to get input from valuable employees	To get quick results from a highly motivated and competent team	To help an employee improve performance or develop long-term strengths
Overall impact on climate	Negative	Most strongly positive	Positive	Positive	Negative	Positive

Here is an example of a leadership philosophy and leadership style that I share with any team member who joins my businesses today:

Leadership Philosophy

The best leaders aren't followed, they're joined.

Leadership Style

Collaborative, fairly hands-on at first (for learning purposes), focused on achieving results as a team and developing you

The philosophy is a quote I came up with a while back which encompasses the meaning of servant-leadership in my mind. I actually wrote a whole chapter about it in Rule #13.

My leadership style is a combination of Democratic and Coaching from Goleman's Six Leadership Styles we mentioned. I am fairly hands-on with new employees or when I first take over a team. I never want to be the only person making decisions, but would rather empower my team members to make decisions for two reasons— (1) to increase their buy-in to the vision and ownership of the results and (2) to develop them professionally. Notice I did not use the terms *democratic* and *coaching* in my leadership-style explanation for my team. It is more for my self-awareness as a leader and I realize the words mean nothing to them.

Now, take a few moments to draft your leadership philosophy and leadership style. This can also be downloaded from my website (www.ravensolomon.com) under the **Leading Your Parents** tab, Resources section, or found in the **Leading Your Parents** workbook releasing in May 2019.

Drafting Your Leadership Philosophy

Define leadership in your own words.

_____

_____

_____

_____

GIVE A PROPER INTRODUCTION

Who is the best leader you know?

_____

_____

_____

_____

What are some of the characteristics you admire about that person?

_____

_____

_____

_____

What leadership quote resonates with you most and why?

_____

_____

_____

_____

After reflecting on your answers to the above questions, take a stab at your one to two sentence leadership philosophy. This simply articulates what leadership is to you.

_____

_____

_____

Communicating Your Leadership Style

Review the chart above to determine which of the six leadership styles best reflect you own. You can select two at the most.

What are some single words that describe your style?

_____

_____

_____

_____

Why do you think this style best represents your own?

_____

_____

_____

_____

In your own words, write a brief description of your leadership style, suitable for a slide.

_____

_____

_____

_____

_____

Similar to what I did under the example above, write a paragraph explaining exactly what you would say to verbally describe your leadership style.

_____

_____

_____

_____

_____

_____

_____

_____

Step 4: Tell Them what They can Expect

What do they need to know about your personal expectations? What time do you typically arrive in the office? Will you be working extra hours to get caught up-to-speed in your new role? What is your plan to get to your team? Do you plan on scheduling one-on-one meetings with each of them? What is the cadence for team meetings? How about one-on-one meetings? What are your default methods of communication? How should they handle problems that may arise right now, as you get acclimated? Is there a training schedule for you which might make you inaccessible for large amounts of time?

Depending on several factors, there are many things you can cover on this slide. You are more than capable of using sound judgement to determine what is best given your specific circumstances. The truth is, they probably feel quite a bit of anxiety about having a new leader. You goal on this slide is to ease some of that anxiety by answering as many of their unexpressed questions about the unknown as possible.

Step 5: Ask Them what They Expect

This slide really should be empty, with nothing but the question or a question mark. At this point of the meeting, you stop talking and listen attentively. You ask one very important question that I promise you they will remember you delivering as long as you are their leader. **What are your expectations of me?** If they are anything like my first team, they will take it from there! LOL. If they don't, pose a few probing questions. What are their expectations when it comes to management? What do they expect when it comes to approvals? And of course, let's not forget communication.

That's right, this is the perfect time to have the conversation we mentioned earlier about communication preferences and plans. Depending on how much time you have, you may be able to hash out the plan on the spot, but more than likely you'll just listen and take notes. You'll want to ask questions like, *What modes of communication do you prefer and why? How has communication amongst the team been in the past? What worked well? What didn't work well? What changes would you make to the way information is communicated today? What do you think the results would be if we improved our communication?*

Take notes, and after the meeting, spend time digesting them and thinking through your 30-60-90 Day Plan—What do you want to accomplish in your first 30 days, first 60 days and first 90 days? Do you need a template for that too? You know I've got your back! Just head over to my website (www.ravensolomon.com), visit the ***Leading Your Parents*** tab and download a template I've built just for you from the Resources section!

RULE #6: WORK HARD

#hardwork

#resilience

Now that you've introduced yourself to your team and have explained to them how great you will be for them, it's now time to live up to those promises. For more than one reason, it's now time to work your butt off.

The first is the pre-established value system some of your team members hold. As we covered in Rule #2, Traditionalists, the generation preceding the Baby Boomers, and Baby Boomers themselves, are known to value hard work in the workplace. As you seek to gain their trust and respect, it is important to speak their language, if you will, and display a value that is so important to them.

The second reason is quite simple, and a little selfish—you have a lot to learn! As with marriage, said by many, the first year on any new job is the toughest. In some roles, you can literally spend the entire first year learning the ins and outs of the job, not to mention the culture and the people with whom you work. However, most places of employment don't give you a year to watch the game from the bench before you're expected to play. Instead, you're expected to learn as you play. That calls for some long days—working after hours and starting before hours. Learning new systems, building systems of your own, learning the foundations of the business, spending time with your team members, meetings, interviews, customer relations and so much more. You will have to work hard just to stay afloat. But this year is the foundation of your professional career. You want it to be strong and time well-spent.

I remember my first year as a District Manager fresh out of college. I'd watch my peers—who'd been doing this for what seemed like forever—and long for the level of efficiency they had and the handle they appeared to have on their business. What would take me hours took them minutes. The decisions I labored over they could make with the snap of the finger. Some of the time this would motivate me, and other times it would discourage the heck out of me. However, the reality was they'd put in the time—enough time to learn the business cold. I couldn't expect to have the same level of efficiency they had, having only put in a fraction of the time and effort. I couldn't expect the fruits of my labor to be as sweet, having only labored days as compared to their years, if not decades.

Too often, we Millennials see the end result of years of hard work and think we should be able to have those same results if we work hard, too. And we will. We'll likely have them quicker than the generations before us, but we cannot expect that to be only a year or two.

The third reason is just as simple as the prior—you simply have to earn your keep. I know you don't like the idea that you have to earn your position after you already hold it, but in the eyes of many, you do.

Many people, team members included, will see you as a "kid with a piece of paper," a degree, who got your position based solely on your age. I know, I know…that's not fair! You worked hard for your degree. You learned a lot and have much to bring to the table. You've had two internships and worked a part-time job in college!

I get it. But the reality is, in their world, in their office, you have zero experience. And that's okay. You will indeed learn, apply your degree, and be successful…eventually. But right now, you are starting at the bottom of the totem pole. Act like it. Work hard. Grind! Earn the position you have. Everyday, remind your superiors that they made the right decision by selecting you for this role.

In an earlier chapter, we talked about the importance of humility when starting a new job. Working hard is another way to demonstrate that humility. It conveys the message that nothing is beneath you.

I can recall my days on the route truck like they were yesterday. I would get in around 5 a.m. to pick up my truck and handheld device and get back around 6 p.m. with an empty truck. I wouldn't stop working until the truck was empty, after every delivery was made and every customer was satisfied. *Every day.* The knees in all of my pants were faded from working bottom shelves and my shirts were absolutely filthy by the end of each day. My shoes looked like I'd been working in them for a year and my fanny pack (yes, fanny pack!) was always on the side of my hip so it remained out of my way. I was WORKING. Working HARD.

I made sure the condition of all of my stores was stellar. Every bag was rotated, every store had adequate stock, the shelves look popped and ready and all product was fresh and safe for consumption. This was not because I was worried someone from management would come into the stores for which I was responsible and check my work, but because I wanted to do a good job. I wanted to earn my keep and I wasn't afraid to get dirty and work hard to do it.

This hard work didn't go unnoticed. Unbeknownst to me, there was conversation going on around the dock (amongst the other route salespeople) about my work ethic. There was conversation amongst my future peers about my work ethic. And most importantly, and also unbeknownst to me, there were conversations being shared with my boss about my work ethic. See guys, I mentioned earlier that a first impression is extremely hard to undo. The first impression I gave to the entire group around me, simply through my hard work, was one of diligence, determination and excellence. When I finished the route portion of my training and came into the office, my name had already preceded me.

Your name will precede you, too. The question is, what will be said?

Please know that you are being observed and conversations are indeed being shared about you during all segments of your career. You would be surprised to know how many. Between the frontline, your peers, your management and the support staff, your name is often being mentioned. It typically starts out with a, "Hey, how's _____ doing?" or, "How's it going with _____?"

You control the narrative, my friend. Work hard, so those conversations speak of the right things.

While we are speaking of hard word, I would like to address my ladies for just one second. Be honest, ladies—have you ever played the *damsel in distress*? You know, when you act completely helpless in a situation so a man can swoop in as a hero to save the day? Yes—that damsel. I am instructing you to let her die. Let the damsel die!

As a leader, it is absolutely okay to ask for help. In fact, sometimes it's admirable to do so. However, when you consistently play this helpless role just to get people to do things for you, it may be seen as cute by some (namely the guys helping you) but it is not admirable and will likely take away from the respect they have for you as a leader. When you consistently portray yourself as incapable in an area, that area may become you in total. And it is much easier for people who already speculate whether you should be here or not based on your age to very quickly develop that viewpoint. Playing the damsel in distress role fuels their speculation and gives them another reason to deem you incapable of being their leader. Let the damsel die!

Let me give you an example of playing the damsel in distress versus simply asking for a hand. There is a box of supplies a few inches out of your reach. There is a communal stepladder a few feet away but you decide to go grab your team member, who is finishing up his paperwork for the day, to come and grab the box for you. While your goal is to make him feel needed, you actually made yourself look lazy. You could have definitely grabbed the stepladder and gotten the box yourself, perhaps in the same amount of time it took you to go find your team member and bring him back to help. If there were no stepladder, this would have been a case of simply asking for a quick hand.

Here's the key indicator that you are playing the damsel in distress role and not just asking for help: You are fully capable of and have all the necessary tools to perform the task but you ask for *help*.

Body language and tone also matter tremendously when identifying our damsel in distress tendencies. Tilting your head to the side, playing with your hair, speaking in the soft, whiney voice and pouting are all things we do when seeking to get our way as a damsel. These behaviors are unacceptable for the workplace and even more so with subordinates. I am aware some of these men may be old enough to be your father and oftentimes we get what we want from Dad by doing such things. These men are not your dad, this is not home and you are not a little girl. You are a leader who's been selected to take your team to the next level.

Playing the damsel in distress may get you help in the moment, but it most certainly will not earn you respect or promotion in the long run. You want to be taken seriously and be respected as a leader. Sure, you may not be as physically strong or tall so you may, indeed, need a hand here and there with a few things, but please—let the damned damsel die and show you aren't afraid of a little hard work!

RULE #7: DISPLAY CONFIDENCE

#selfconfidence
#bodylanguage
#nonverbalcommunication
#assertion

The word on the street is we Millennials and Centennials have no problem displaying self-confidence because we think we know it all anyway. Perhaps that is true for you, but it is not true for me—not when I've been leading people with more years in the workplace than my years on earth! Nope, I'm not immediately confident. Not at all. But, even if I'm not, it's important that I display that I am.

I know, I know…just a few chapters ago I was telling you to be humble and display humility, and now I'm telling you to display confidence. "What do you want from me!?" you're probably screaming. Let me explain.

The display of confidence I'm speaking of is an assurance in your capability versus your ability. See, your capability is what you are capable of doing in the future, while your ability is what you are able to do now. If you were not capable, you wouldn't have the job. But just because you're capable doesn't mean you are able just yet. That's where the humility comes in. Does that make sense? In other words, you are confident they selected the right person and that you will knock this job out of the park, but you are humble enough to know that you don't know everything it takes to do that *just yet*. This is reason both to hold your head up high and keep your spirit meek.

Do you remember the concept of being **confidently humble**, from our chapter on humility? To be so comfortable in a place of humility that you actually exude confidence? Well, the type of confidence I'm speaking of in this chapter is not quite the same thing. This confidence is more tangible and defined. It's more like just plain old, traditional confidence....using body language.

Have you ever heard an elder tell you to look them in the eyes when talking to them? If you haven't, then I will be that elder for you today. Always make eye-contact with any and everyone you speak with! You should do this everywhere, but it is especially important to do so in professional environments, and even more for leaders. Making and maintaining eye-contact during a conversation is one sure way to display confidence.

There are countless studies that support the effectiveness of eye-contact in leadership and overall communication. According to a study from the Idiap Research Institute[1] eye-contact shows a person's social hierarchy and dominance in a conversation. People at the top of the chain of command tend to look longer at their subject and they receive more eye-contact in return.

In her book **The Body Language Advantage**[2], body language expert Lillian Glass notes the importance of eye-contact, saying that breaking eye-contact not only suggests submissiveness, but that, "when eye-contact is maintained, it signifies control or power over a situation and establishes dominance." In other words, it displays confidence.

Another study[3] found that participants with higher self-esteem break eye-contact less frequently, whereas those with lower self-esteem break eye-contact more frequently.

Need any more evidence that eye-contact matters, especially in leadership?

If you don't consistently make eye-contact today, chances are incorporating this new body language might feel awkward for you. If you are particularly uncomfortable staring into someone's eyes, here are a few tips:

1. Look at the bridge of the nose- The other person will not be able to tell you are not actually looking at their eyes. Even looking at the mouth will be a seamless difference to the average converser.

2. Focus on one eye- This is actually far more common than trying to focus both of your eyes on both the eyes of another person.

3. Practice- You can practice in the mirror, on Facetime, using YouTube or the television.

Another way to display confidence through your body language is to always give a firm handshake. A HUGE pet peeve of mine is a flimsy handshake. You don't have to squeeze the circulation out of the person's limb, but you should certainly apply a little tension and use the whole hand, not just your fingertips. A simple tip is to imagine yourself flexing your muscles as you shake someone's hand. It doesn't take intensive squeezing to flex your muscles, just a little bit of focused energy. That is what you want to apply when shaking someone's hand.

Ladies, this applies to you at least as much, if not more so. Just because you're a woman doesn't mean you should have a dainty handshake. If you are leading men, let them know who's boss through your handshake. Let them know you mean business. A firm handshake doesn't make you less feminine or more masculine. It simply sends a message of confidence. I've had men from all parts of business comment on my handshake. Most of the time it's stuff like, "Firm handshake you've got there, young lady," or "Wow, a lady with a handshake…I like it!" It's nice to hear but with or without that verbal affirmation, I know it's an important and effective cue to send.

To that end, making eye-contact while shaking someone's hand is extremely effective, as well, as it displays comfort and warmth, thus making the other person relaxed.

Posture is another way to use your body to display confidence. Some other body language cues include sitting up versus slouching and walking with your head and chest up and your shoulders relaxed. Notice I said chest up and not out. Out would be boastful, prideful and arrogant. Up is attentive and present.

Avoid fiddling with objects as you speak or listen, such as your clothing, name badge, phone, bag, etc. It communicates nervousness or anxiety as well as a lack of confidence in what you are saying or will say.

You may think I'm giving frivolous advice about things that don't matter in the grand scheme of things, but that couldn't be further from the truth. All of these body language tips feed a very important thing for corporate success called ***executive presence***, something most people don't learn about until several years into their careers, if ever. *Executive presence* is pretty much the corporate term for swag, LOL. It's the ability to take command of a room with your presence alone—exuding confidence, poise and composure. Practicing these body language tips as you begin your career will put you steps ahead of the pack and catch the eye of leadership. Companies spend millions coaching executives, or potential executives, how to have presence. It's *that* important.

If you want to one day be an executive, get a jumpstart on the competition and practice displaying confidence, or presence, in your leading. I promise you, decision-makers are looking for it.

I was 28 years old when I became an executive at my first employer, which I had been with for about 6.5 years at the time. I knew I was young for an executive-level position and so did everyone else—my team and their teams included—but I also knew I could do the job. With my confidence in my capabilities, I carried myself like I ran the show. I'm not sure how I ranked on the *confidently humble* scale, but I certainly displayed confidence and had presence. That actually leads me to a good point. As you rise in the organization, the need to be confidently humble decreases, in my opinion. Unlike entering into a managerial position straight out of college, by the time you reach the executive level, respect is somewhat innate and people actually do think you know everything, or at least should. Okay, maybe not EVERYthing but you get what I'm saying. As a new manager, you are confidently humble in the fact that you are new and don't know everything. As a new executive, you are confident that you know the business and simply have to get to know the ins and outs of the people and unique challenges of this particular organization. I knew the business and just needed to get to know the intricacies of this particular piece of the business and try to learn as much about 300 people and 2,000 customers as I could.

Back to my body language. I looked every frontline team member I met square in the eye, delivered a firm handshake, greeted them by repeating their names and reinforced my concern for them by a reassuring pat on the back (literally) or a tap on the arm. I was always dressed like I was the boss, which we will discuss a little later, and I even wore loud shoes that reinforced my presence. I have to be honest—the loud shoes weren't purposeful, but one day I received some feedback from a frontline team member that made me realize there was actually a connection being made with the sound of loud shoes and my presence. I immediately thought of what I call the *principal effect*.

As a school kid, do you remember being in the classroom and hearing the loud *clack* of shoes, high-heels, precisely, coming down the empty hallways? Who did you immediate think it was? The principal, of course—the highest authoritative figure in the building. You would immediately sit up in your seat and pretend (or not) to be intently focused on the lesson being delivered by your favorite teacher in the whole wide world. Do you also remember the feelings associated with that noise? Maybe it was fear, maybe it was admiration, but it was most certainly respect.

I quickly learned that something as small as the shoes I wore played a role in my body language. Now, some may argue that I was sending the wrong message with *principal effect* shoes—a message of dominating power. I would say as a newly-appointed 28-year-old African American female executive in a male-dominated industry where the median age is likely 8-10 years older than me, the non-verbal message of confidence and who is in charge could not be too loud.

To become more well-versed in body language, there are tons of books out there you can read or videos you can watch. I'm sure they are great, but to be honest with you, the way I best learned my non-verbal cues was by simple observation. I observed the way my manager interacted with his/her team and frontline employees. (If you haven't noticed yet, I don't like using the term subordinates. Albeit accurate by definition, I find it to be a derogatory term.) As I got more exposure to senior leaders, I observed the way they interacted with me and my peers, and even my team members. I watched how the Vice Presidents and C-Suite executives made me feel like I was the center of their attention, if but for a moment, and that they cared about my success. Most of the time we remember our bad encounters with senior leaders, but I challenge you to pay close attention to and remember your good ones. They are walking, breathing manuals for what you more than likely desire to be—and make no mistake about it, they did not get there based solely upon their technical abilities.

RULE #8: GO BY THE BOOK

#accountability
#consistency
#performancemanagement
#takingcriticism

Did you have strict parents growing up? I sure did! Goodness! I wasn't allowed to do much of anything and I hated it. In the inspirational keynotes I often make to students, I tell the story of living while in grade school with my grandmother, who'd recently retired. We all lived there—my mother, sister, brother and I—in her two-bedroom home on the west side of Charlotte, NC. My mom worked really hard to provide the most she could for us and my grandmother took on most of the in-home responsibilities like cooking and caring for us after school. We lived in a drug-infested neighborhood filled with a lot of bad things and that was no secret to anyone. However, as a child, all I wanted to do was go play and run in the streets like the other kids. But mom and grandma knew best and there was no getting around them.

It wasn't until I got off of the bus one day during a drug bust that I realized there was an infamous drug house on the corner of our street. The house the bus dropped me in front of every single day was full of drugs, prostitution, dealers and junkies. I'd had no idea.

My siblings and I pushed for new freedoms all the time, but my grandmother and mother never gave in. They knew the dangers and refused to let us go beyond the front yard. The only social outlet I had after school was the library across the street. It was less than a mile away from the house, but my grandmother would NOT let me walk. She would literally drive me the mile! After the drug bust, I understood why. Rarely could I hang out with my friends and go to the skating rink, movies, etc.

Now that I'm all grown up, having excelled in college and my career the way I have, I am grateful for the strict approach my grandmother and mother took in parenting me. I'm glad they were stern and no-nonsense, holding me accountable to fulfill my potential as a high-achiever. I'm glad they saw the potential impact the people I was hanging around might have had on my future. They were good people...we just weren't headed in the same direction.

I share this story with you because as a leader, you are going to have to be the unpopular one like my grandmother, who sees past the gripes and complaints of your team members and holds them to the standard of excellence you know they are capable of producing. This may be hard, but the long-term benefits for both parties outweigh the short-term discomfort in the beginning.

Most people think they want an easy boss. And who knows, maybe they really do—but if that's the case, I can assure you it is because they have become complacent and have no interest in growing. They just want to be left alone, produce *good enough* and avoid the chopping block. That's it. You may have a few people on your team like this. But for those who desire to grow—professionally and personally—they really don't want an easy boss. They want a boss who is going to make them better, stronger and ready for the next level. Just like I thought I wanted easy parents so I could do what I wanted to do, what I really needed were stern parents who would bring out the best in me long-term. Now I adore and praise them constantly for the sternness they'd applied in raising me because it's made me who I am today.

Are you willing to defer your adoration and appreciation as a leader? Would you rather be liked now because you're easy or appreciated later because you were tough?

I was a fairly tough boss when it came to effort. I believe that except for extenuating outside factors, there are usually only two reasons people fail—a lack of knowledge or a lack of effort. It is always the leader's job to remove lack of knowledge as a barrier. It is your job to inform, educate and lead, equipping your team with the resources necessary to be successful. In part, it is also your job to inspire effort and to motivate the team towards action. I say *in part* because much of someone's effort comes from within. As a leader, I can influence it, but I can't control it. Only the team member can do that. And because of that reality, I challenged my team to consistently put forth the effort to be excellent. That meant thorough feedback on their performance, consistent support (or what we called "work-withs") to coach (remove lack of knowledge as a barrier), and doing anything within my power to make their jobs easier. But sometimes even all of that doesn't work.

I remember my first time I had to write up a team member, issuing formal discipline to go into their file as a part of the performance management process. This particular employee was not performing a key part of the job and was therefore costing the company unnecessary expenses. Okay, I'll stop talking in code! He wasn't rotating product (putting the freshest product at the back of the shelf and the pre-existing product up front), which was causing product to go bad unnecessarily. It was an ongoing issue, one we'd had several conversations and "work-withs" about, and the problem simply boiled down to a lack of effort—laziness. We'd talked about it so many times, I'd coached through it so many times, that it was finally time to take the next step. This employee was known for being...how should I say it...whiney! He was known for kicking up a fuss, jumping the chain of command, and complaining constantly when he wasn't getting his way. Frankly, I didn't care. I knew I had the right rationale and backing to issue the discipline and I hoped it would make him better.

As imagined, he definitely kicked up a fuss, went to my boss to complain and had an attitude with me for a while. When the opportunity presented itself, he moved to another team.

Fast forward about a year and a half. By this time, I'd already moved to a different team, same job, same location, and had now been promoted to a higher position which had relocated me to South Carolina. I was a few months into the job when I received an email from an external address. Guess who it was? You betcha… the first employee I'd ever written up—the one who'd resented me so much for that, that he moved to a different team. He was writing to give me an update. He went on to thank me for holding him accountable many months ago, for believing in him and for requiring more of him than mediocrity. He told me how proud he was of his route now. That it was rotated and much easier to manage. That he's now becoming a leader amongst his peers and is training new hires to run routes the right way. He said that while my by-the-book approach sometimes frustrated them back then, they missed it around there and now realize how healthy it was for the work group. They'd realized I was fair, consistent and clearly cared. He wished me the best and encouraged me not to change.

I could have burst into to tears right there on the spot! In fact, I probably did and don't remember. What a full-circle moment! I had NO idea that my decision to hold this person accountable would push him towards greatness. I had no idea that one day he would appreciate it, just as I now appreciate my grandmother's strict approach. I had no idea. But now that I do, I can advise you with assurance that being consistent, being fair, and being by-the-book (reasonably) will gain you respect and appreciation in the long run. I can tell you that deferred appreciation feels so much better than being popular in the moment. In my experience, being popular isn't a job qualification or critical skill. Making the tough decision to hold people accountable, even when it's unpopular, is.

Listen to what the book says. You can never go wrong going by it and over time you will learn how to add some heart to it.

RULE #9: BE CONSISTENTLY CONSISTENT

#dependability
#reliability
#personalbranding
decisionmaking
#performancemanagement

Acting "by the book" is ineffective if you only do it a portion of the time. If you dare to be a leader who leads *according* to the book, you have to be consistent and lead that way all the time. Holding one person to the fire, while letting another escape for the same offense is poor leadership, may be seen as favoritism and is considered untrustworthy behavior. My best advice, therefore, is to be consistent in your leadership style, including but certainly not limited to accountability.

There are several areas in which you need to be consistent as a leader, but we will focus on these three:

- The way you treat people

- The decisions you make
- The message you convey (via your actions, brand, presence etc.)

THE WAY YOU TREAT PEOPLE

Have you ever come across a leader who clearly had favorites on his or her team? Whether it's in sports, school, work or home, we've all come across a person a time or two who appears to treat one person better than another. Maybe for you, it was a parent. Little Sis could get away with murder, but if you even so much as said the wrong thing, you got scolded. Since we're thinking about it, how did that make you feel? Sad? Unjustly penalized? Dismissed?

Imagine the business implications of a team member working with those types of feelings stemming from their leader. Morale goes down, productivity goes down, targets are missed, quality of work decreases and so much more. For business reasons alone, it is therefore important to be consistent in the way you treat people. But of course, there is also a moral case for consistency.

The Golden Rule, as I'm sure you've heard, says, "Treat people the way you want to be treated." *People* means all people, not just some. Not just your favorites, not just the ones who perform well and don't give you headaches, but *all* people. To take it a step further, the Platinum Rule says, "Treat people the way *they* want to be treated."

That makes leading people even more complex, doesn't it? Absolutely! Only the best of leaders master the platinum. For you, being newer to leadership, I would say let's start with leading by the Golden Rule, with the Platinum as a mid-to-long-term goal.

In either case, treating people fairly, honestly and respectfully is the right thing to do. None of us want to be treated unfairly, and the reality is, we lose respect for people who treat us unfairly. Treat people how you want to be treated and do it consistently.

THE DECISIONS YOU MAKE

The decisions you make as a leader almost always impact your team. It is therefore vital for them to be able to trust you and your decision-making abilities. One way to demonstrate capability when it comes to sound decision-making is to be consistent. After about six-to-nine months of working with you, your team should be able to predict your decisions in relating matters because you're so consistent. You think about the same factors and you ask the same questions.

I remember being a second-year manager, sitting in my one-on-one meetings with my team, being presented with the same problem week after week—displays not being executed. The conversation would consistently go as follows:

> Team Member: We're having a big problem in store 347. Every time I go in there, they've taken down my display!

Me: Okay. That certainly is a problem. Why do they keep removing the displays?

Team Member: I don't know. I'm just sick of it. Every day I have to drag it back out to the sales floor and it's creating more work for me.

Me: Who've you spoken to about the problem?

Team Member: The receiver.

Me: Whom else have you spoken with?

Team Member: No one. She makes all the decisions.

Me: Given that she has a boss, who has a boss, who also has a boss, I think there may be a few more decision-makers in the building. Speak with the Assistant Manager or Store Manager tomorrow and follow up with me, please? Now, how are we doing in your Harris Teeter....

After having that same exact conversation four or five times, before I knew it, I was no longer having conversations about receivers being the barrier to our execution. This team member began to predict my response, and knew he needed a difference excuse, on a different level.

This example relates to communication, but I could throw out countless examples of corrective action and discipline, as well. If I walked into a store and noticed freshness policies were not being followed on one route, we'd have a conversation. The next time it happened, we'd have a documented conversation. The third time, we'd move to the first step in corrective action. Three formal steps could lead to termination. If I walked onto another route with that same issue, the same exact process was followed, with the only difference being where they currently were in the corrective-action procession I just described. The same issues warrant a similar response.

Imagine you committed the same breach of the rules as your peer 30 days apart. All else being equal, the boss decides you deserve to be written up for your breach, but 30 days earlier had decided your peer should only get a warning. One day the breach was worthy of formal discipline, the next day it was not. What kind of message does that send to you and the balance of the team? *Inconsistency illustrates instability. Instability makes it difficult to trust.*

THE MESSAGE YOU CONVEY

Some of the most successful brands in the world have the simplest messages. The simpler the message, the easier it is for consumers to remember and for employees to embody. Let's take a look at a few:

- Apple- Think Different.
- Nike- Just Do It.
- Burger King- Have it Your Way.
- Microsoft- Be What's Next.
- Adidas- Impossible Is Nothing.

Notice they are all very simple but speak directly to the way in which the company desires to position itself in the industry. Apple wants to be the brand that inspires you to *think differently*, while Nike inspires you to overcome your doubts and *just do it*. Burger King wants you to *have it your way*, while Microsoft wants you to *be what's next in the world*. Adidas reminds you *impossible is not a thing*. Do you see how three simple words can communicate so much to the consumer, creating an expectation?

Also, notice how consistent companies keep their brands. It's always the same message, presented over and over again. It's all about building trust.

Your team members are the consumers of your leadership. Is the message you send to them every day clear, concise and consistent? Or is it convoluted, drawn out and unpredictable?

The above examples are slogans, which play a key role in brand messaging for a company. I, and most of the professional world, believe that leaders in the workplace are personal brands themselves. The message you convey is just as important as the message the company you work for conveys.

With that said, should you have a slogan or brand statement? Yes! Unlike brands that are companies, your slogan or brand statement will not necessarily be shared and plastered on everything you do. It's really unspoken and conveyed through your actions—the way you treat people, the decisions you make, the way you present yourself and more. For that reason, personal branding can sometimes be harder than branding a company.

Your slogan or brand statement as a leader doesn't have to be three words, but it needs to be that clear and simple to you—something you can almost put into three-to-five simple words. For example, *Always there.*

WHY BE CONSISTENT?

Being consistent, above all, makes it easier for your team members to trust you. There is some degree of predictability with you which makes them feel comfortable. Even if they don't like the result, they at least know what that result will be. As a kid, If I misbehaved at school, I knew my grandmother or mother would be waiting at home with a switch for me. I hated the result but I knew it was coming. And the fact that this same discipline applied to both of my siblings made it fair.

Secondly, fair and consistent leaders earn respect of their PSS (Peers, Superiors and Subordinates).

Third, consistency makes for easier measurements and makes my data more trustworthy. If I'm measuring policy compliance, for example, and sometimes I let breaches slide while other times I take action, my data is unreliable.

Fourthly, I don't know about you, but being consistently consistent gives me peace. I sleep well at night knowing I was fair in the way I've treated people, the decisions I've made, and the messages I conveyed.

Lastly, consistent behaviors create consistent results.

RULE #10: DO THE LITTLE THINGS

#emotionalintelligence
#socialawareness
#executivepresence
#relationshipmanagement

Your team will naturally pay attention to everything you do. They've probably been frustrated with much of the leadership they had in the past, so it is all too easy to question whether their manager cares about them or not.

This is especially true if you are coming into management like I did, fresh out of college and a little wet behind the ears. Your team will be asking themselves, "Is she in this for the long-haul, or is she simply ticking off a box, looking for promotions?" As unfair as it may seem, it's your duty to counter the doubt, fear and frustration they've accumulated from working with past leadership. You must build trust and rapport with them.

In order to do this, you need to know what matters the most to your team members. You need to know the big things in their lives so that you can do the little things in your leadership to really make a difference.

So, how do you learn about those big things? How do you find out what really matters to your team? This is a very complex strategy, so listen up.

Are you ready?

YOU ASK THEM!

Yes, it is that simple. Set some time aside to get to know each of your team members one-by-one. Talk to them about business, but also about their lives. Get to know them not only as professionals but as people. Schedule and spend an entire day with each of them, experiencing the business from their perspectives and chatting in your downtime.

I know, I know...it seems a bit counterintuitive. As leaders, we are constantly prioritizing an endless list of action items, and sitting with an employee seems at first glance like it would be pretty low on the list. But it's not. Or at least, it shouldn't be. There is an absolute business case for building trust and rapport with your team. In **Watson Wyatt's** 2002 study[1], high-trust organizations outperformed low-trust organizations in total return to shareholders by **286%**. It may seem like your small relationship with an employee is miniscule when it comes to establishing a culture of high trust within your organization, but I would beg to differ. You and your team ARE the culture and you set the tone daily. The **Franklin Covey** organization says it best—

> *"When trust is high, the resulting dividend you receive is like a performance multiplier, elevating and improving every dimension of your organization and your life. Trust increases value, accelerates growth, enhances innovation, improves collaboration, strengthens partnerships, increases execution and heightens loyalty."*[2]

Invest time into your personal relationships with the people you lead and do it right away. Lay a foundation of trust during this initial interaction and allow every decision you make to follow through on a promise, to be a brick of trust added, until you have a solid structure indestructible by any outside force.

Here's how you start: The first time you sit down with any employee one-on-one, begin by taking notes. It may seem a bit weird to show up with a notebook, but the fact of the matter is, you're probably not going to remember everything and it's vitally important that you do.

Secondly, you want them to know you're listening and are serious about the things they are expressing, be it personal or professional. Ask them when their birthday is, the name of their dog, how old their kids are and what hobbies they enjoy outside of work. Your goal is to learn the big things that matter to them so that you can show that you care by doing the *little things*.

For example, someone's spouse is a big deal to them. You, as their manager, asking about their spouse is a little thing you can do to show you care about that team member as a person, not just as an employee. Remembering the spouse's name adds a special, personal touch which will make them think, *Wow! She or he really listened to me.*

People appreciate the little things. It's human nature.

Ask your team members what keeps them up at night about their jobs. Ask them what they liked or didn't like about their previous manager. Ask them what their expectations are of you—so you know what to give them! Yes, you've already posed this question to the team, but perhaps there is more a team member didn't feel comfortable sharing in front of the group. Let the conversation flow organically from there. The more sincere you are around the questions you ask, the more they will open up and let you in. Beware, however. Once you're in, like a gardener, you are responsible for what grows and dies there. You have the power to heal wounds left by other leaders, but you also have the power to make wounds bigger. Steward this opportunity carefully. This is why follow-up and follow-through are so important. We will cover that thoroughly later.

I remember my first couple of weeks as a new manager. As you now know probably all too well, my team drove chip trucks, delivering every type of chip imaginable to every drug store, big-box retailer (like Sam's Club) and everything in between. They'd start as early as 3 a.m. and end as late as 7 p.m., sometimes later. It was my desire to spend some quality time with them as a new leader and the reality was, there was no way that would happen except by hopping on the truck with them and spending a full day, side-by-side, throwing up chips. I'd dust off my route clothes, throw on my fanny pack—which seem to be making a comeback now—pull down that God awful fold-up chair over the steps of their box truck and we were off! 3 a.m. or 7 a.m. It didn't matter. My goal was to spend time and listen.

They told me about their children, their partners, their grandchildren. They told me their birthdays (minus the year) and their upcoming vacation plans. They told me about their frustrations with the company and the job itself. They told me what they loved about their old boss and what they hated. We put up chips, ate, laughed, argued, put up more chips and just talked. I enjoyed hearing about them and made sure I took notes.

One thing I didn't do very well was let them into my life the way they'd let me into theirs. The truth was, I didn't have any kids or grandkids or a boyfriend, and I felt I really had very little to talk about. If I could do it all over again, I'd probably dig a little deeper and open up more. The point is, I learned about what mattered most to my team members and I made sure I did as many little things as possible to show them I heard them and that I cared.

So what are some of those little things I'm speaking of?

- Writing personalized, handwritten notes for birthdays and other special occasions
- Remembering and using the names of those they love—children, grandchildren, partners, pets, etc.
- Discussing their hobbies, even if they're not your own
- Removing obstacles they'd mentioned to make their jobs easier
- Choosing a place for lunch that adheres to their diet
- Remember and celebrate their work anniversary
- Be present during your time with them (we talk more about this in Rule #14)
- Ask their opinion
- Take notes when they are speaking to you
- Ask how they are doing and truly listen to their answers

Your team must hear this message from you consistently:

I'm listening, I am concerned, I am here... for you.

BEAT YOUR OWN EXPECTATIONS

As a sales manager with F&B, there were many days where my team had a full workload and needed help to manage it all. If I didn't have any extra personnel to send their way, I'd step in to help.

If I said I was going to show up at 9 a.m., I was there, whether my team member had arrived yet or not. If it cost me an hour to build a display for them to relieve their workload, I spent that hour.

If they asked me for plastic caddies in which to carry small items like sunflower seeds and peanuts, which were usually somewhere in a huge warehouse that would probably take them a half-an-hour to find, I spent the time scouring to make sure the next day those caddies were found and in their breakroom with their names written on them. When leading a team, it's vital that every second be maximized as much as possible, and eliminating cumbersome tasks from your team's plate is important. It may seem like an inconsequential thing to you as a manager, but a millisecond may make a world of difference to them.

I once had an employee who showed up to work sick. He looked pretty bad but kept saying, "I'll push through it." I notice that when guys are sick, they don't always feel comfortable asking for help, especially not from female managers. Maybe I'm looking too deep into that—I don't know. I was so grateful he'd come in to work because there was no way I could have run his route for him that day. But I suspected he would need some help, so I cleared out the back half of my day and later showed up on his route.

Before I continue this story, I should give a little context. At F&B Company, the person running the route—each team member— not only drives the truck and delivers the product to every 7-11, Walgreens and Walmart along the way, they also have to stock the shelves and displays inside of each store. And if it were a holiday week where more snacks are consumed than average, there would potentially be displays all over the store.

In this case my team member was struggling and had even pulled over a few times on his route to be sick. To help him, I told him to simply drop the product off at each store and keep going. As opposed to him putting the product on the shelves, I would come up behind him and take care of that part, which was by far the toughest part. He was shocked but extremely grateful.

That's how I was raised. My mom was the type of person who would simply do whatever needed to get done. Leading isn't just dictating or telling people what to do. It is also your job to fill in the gaps when and where they need to be filled and to make your team members' jobs easier. To me, this is *servant leadership*.

The first time I was exposed to the concept of *servant leadership* was through the scholarship program I was involved in at NC State. At that point, I had never led people, and didn't really think of myself as a leader. As I learned more about *servant leadership*, which was the main pillar of the program, I realized it was the style of leadership which most aligned with my values. To be a servant leader you must have integrity. You are the bottom of the pyramid, not the top.

Some people are intimidated by the name, but just like in this example, servant leadership is really no more than leading by example, which has always resonated with me. I am a self-admitted perfectionist, and because I have such high expectations of others, there was no way I was going to succeed unless I applied those same expectations to myself. If I knew one of my team members needed help or felt they couldn't do the job, then it was my job to step in and beat my own expectations. This was just another little way for me to show them that I listened, I was concerned, and that I was there—for them.

EQ

At its core, doing the little things—showing care and concern—is the demonstration of this thing called *emotional intelligence*. You may or may not have heard of this term before but if you haven't, hopefully you will be familiar enough with it by the end of this book to want to go deeper into it in your own time. It will truly be a game changer in your career.

In short, *emotional intelligence* is the capacity to be aware of, control and express one's emotions and to handle interpersonal relationships judiciously and empathetically.[3] It used to be that a person's intelligence was solely determined by his or her IQ. That was, until two psychologists by the names of **John Mayer** and **Peter Salovey** challenged us to think differently by introducing a concept called emotional intelligence. They suggested there is more to a person's success in life than just their IQ. People also need to have some level of self- awareness, social awareness, self-management and relationship management, according to **Daniel Goleman.** Doing the little things—showing care and concern—is a combination of the social awareness and relationship management aspects all in one.

Contrary to what some believe, I think emotional intelligence can be intentionally learned by anyone. It's like a muscle—we all have it, but it has to be worked and developed.

No matter how big your grand vision is, there are many little things that need to happen to achieve those ends. If you work backward from the goal, somewhere in that framework you'll discover those who are your people.

Your responsibility as a leader is to figure out how to get the most out of each person as an individual. Everybody is different. Some people are just working to collect a paycheck, and that's okay. Others are on a career path and see their job as a means to climbing a corporate ladder. What matters is that you are listening to them and are applying a different approach to each team member.

The key to high productivity lies in the small things. Get into their heads, understand what matters most to them, and make sure even the smallest things are getting done.

RULE #11: DON'T TALK ABOUT IT, BE ABOUT IT

#accountability

#dependability

#reliability #integrity

#selfmanagement

#relationshipmanagement

One of the most important characteristics a leader can have is integrity. Sometimes that word can be a bit vague, so I like to define it quite simply:

> *Integrity is doing what you say you're going to do and being who you say you are.*

That's it. Be a man or woman of your word. Period.

To me, it's just as simple to do as it is to write, but some people really struggle with being a person of integrity. As a leader, however, lacking integrity is a costly gap, as it is vital to good leadership.

Why? Because it is another way to build trust with your team, and we've already talked about how vital trust is in any organization. Doing what you say you're going to do and being who you say you are is a simple, sure way to build that trust.

Integrity can be demonstrated in two simple ways as a leader: *following through* and *following up*. Following through is executing the promises you make. It's doing what you said you would do. Following up is touching base with the ones to whom you've made the promise at a specific time to (a) communicate that the promise was done and (b) ensure both parties' expectations were met.

These two simple things send a powerful and direct message to those you lead. Following through on your commitments tells them they can rely on you to get things done. Following up lets them know they can depend on you to ensure it's done correctly. Both are extremely important messages for your team to hear and believe, but of the two, follow-through is the most important; following up is merely reinforcement. However, because following up is a bit more nuanced, let's address it first.

FOLLOWING UP

Have you ever come across someone who is terrible at following up? They may even do what they said they would do, but their lack of follow-up never informs you so in your eyes it's as if it never happened. Talk about a waste of execution! The bottom line is we can do a lot for people and with people and the value can either be diminished or enhanced by this simple act called *follow-up*.

To **follow up** simply means to check in. It can be done by email, phone, text, social media or quite frankly any mode of communication available. It should remind the person of what was discussed (the reason for the conversation) and provide an update and the layout of the next steps, where applicable. There are tons of reasons to follow up and likely just as many ways to do so, but blindly speaking, those are elements frequently included.

Follow-up is essential in team communication and building trust and so should be done frequently. But is there a such thing as following up too much? The answer is *absolutely!* If done without the proper framework, following up can come across as micromanaging, which can send the dangerous message to your team that you don't trust them. And if you don't trust them, why would they trust you? Because trust is so vital to building a strong relationship with your team, as we've discussed at length now, you want to avoid the feeling of micromanaging at all costs.

To avoid following up too often and making your team members feel micromanaged, I recommend establishing mutual goals and a proper cadence of following up **together**. We'll cover this by looking at what I call the **process of establishing accountability**.

Process of Establishing Accountability

One of your goals as a leader is to build an inclusive team where everyone feels they have a voice, thus taking ownership and initiative. You don't want followers—you want partners, which we'll talk more about in Rule #13. To build an inclusive team, you need open dialogue and shared responsibility. This process of establishing accountability encompasses both and will help you define a suitable follow up process for you.

Process of Establishing Accountability

1. Set the expectation
2. Clarify
3. Determine how you measure results
4. When do we check-in?
5. Consequences/Impact
6. Summarize in writing
7. Brainstorm

For the sake of our attention spans, we'll focus on the steps that are required for effective follow up—Steps 1, 3 and 4.

The first step in the process of establishing accountability is to set clear expectations. You would think, because you're now the sheriff in town, this should be done by you and only you. That is true if you want followers and a top-down leadership style. If you want an inclusive team of partners, you'll need to set expectations **with** your team or individually with team members. Nine-times-out-of-10 you'll have pre-established metrics you're responsible for your team achieving. If the company is really giving their leaders room to be leaders, you won't be given a rubric on **how** to achieve the metrics. That's why they hired you!

The good news is it's not solely your responsibility to figure out the *how*. Allow your team to help. Allow them to provide input into the *how* and then together, set the expectations for everyone to execute the overarching *how* in pursuit of the goal.

Step 2 is to simply clarify or reiterate the decided-upon expectations to ensure everyone understands and are in alignment. This is the time to both answer and pose any questions to your team to ensure all are on the same page.

Now that you've agreed on the expectations and clarified for understanding, Step 3 is collectively determining how progress towards those goals and expectations will be measured. Will it be sales to prior year, profit increases to last quarter, decreased turnover, etc.? Will we look at figures or percentages? And how often? These types of questions are answered in this step.

Once you've agreed there, move on to Step 4, asking the team, "When do you think is a good time to check in and assess our progress?" As long as it's reasonable, **let them determine the cadence**. Here's the teacher in me coming out a bit. Class, why would we want them to establish the cadence of follow-up versus you?

> You: Because it increases their level of buy-in and ownership in the process.
>
> Me: Yes, You! That is exactly right! Why else?

You: Because they can't complain about the follow-up being too frequent and you micromanaging if they've previously determined when you'll check-in.

Me: Exactly, You! You're on fire today!

Now that the cadence has been established, set a reminder in your phone, tablet, or computer to follow up with them at that particular point. As a leader, you also want to make sure it's in their calendars as well. Ask them to follow up with you, as well. Give them permission to hold **you** accountable.

Step 5 consists of making sure both parties understand the consequences if expectations and goals are not met and the impact if they are. Step 6 is to summarize the accountability contract in writing in order for both parties to have a record of it. Sign it if necessary. And lastly, I also like to leave the conversation on a positive foot where possible, so I would suggest spending some time brainstorming on how we will actually achieve our goals and any obstacles in their way I need to remove.

FOLLOWING THROUGH

Now, here's your opportunity to **follow through**. In the case of the process of establishing accountability, actually follow up on the agreed-upon date and carry through on the consequences discussed if the established expectations are not met or the metrics not attained. Following through is just that simple.

As an entrepreneur today, I follow this process with every team member and business partner I have. Everyone owns the goal and the process of achieving. Therefore, we all own the follow-through and follow-up in pursuit.

I know we breezed through the process of establishing accountability, so I've included a full example at the end of this chapter.

Under-Promise, Over-Deliver

I absolutely hate cancelling on people. If I've said it, I want to make it happen, regardless of any obstacles that may arise to make it more difficult, or sometimes even impossible. And if, God forbid, I cannot personally deliver on a promise, I will find someone else who can. To me, it's just decent respect and common courtesy. I understand everyone doesn't see it that way, hence why I felt this was a necessary chapter in this book.

If I can be fully transparent for a moment, I think the importance I put on being reliable and dependable and following through on my promises has a lot to do with my childhood experiences growing up with a drug-addicted parent. My father made some poor decisions in life and unfortunately, the impact was felt by more than just him. Due to his addiction, he made many promises he couldn't keep. I remember what it felt like to be on the receiving end of those broken promises and remember vowing at a young age that unlike him, I would always be a woman of my word—one who kept the promises she made and never forgot what disappointment felt like.

It is perhaps for that reason I make it a point to under-promise and over-deliver in my life, but even more so in my leadership.

You may not have a personal experience that drives you to be dependable, and that is okay. I urge you to do one of two things. (1) Simply tap into the part of you that cares about the feelings of others and be moved to protect those feelings; or (2) Think about what it feels like when people cancel on you. Either of these should drive you towards empathy. Another option can always be to look at your actions completely objectively and see the opportunity costs on your brand for developing a reputation as one who doesn't hold his/her promises. It may cost you a lot in opportunity for advancement, growth and potential business results.

Simply stated, under-promise and over-deliver. When promising, knowing your capacity is key. Before you promise, ensure you have the capacity to execute beyond that promise.

When You Just Can't

Now, every one of us is human. It is impossible to keep all of our promises all the time. To expect that would be completely unreasonable. Things will happen and problems will arise that will sometimes disrupt our plans. So, if you find yourself in a situation where you cannot uphold a commitment, this first thing I suggest is to try to find a replacement or alternate solution before doing anything else. After you've made arrangements, immediately call your boss, customer, team member or whomever is the impacted party. If the reason is personal in nature, tell them as much as you can about it. Confirm with them who is replacing you and if that is okay—if there is anyone replacing you at all. If you weren't able to find a replacement or alternative solution, make it clear that you're working on it. If nobody can cover for you, designate a day in the future when you'll make it up to them and tell them how. In short, communicate, communicate and communicate.

To sum it all up, if you don't follow up and follow through, you lose trust and credibility with your team. We've talked about how important trust is—it's literally the foundation of all relationships. That foundation can be faulty or it can be strong. The decisions you make in things like follow-through and follow-up determine which it will be. Make your team aware that you're paying attention, are willing to hold them and yourself accountable and that you can be relied upon to deliver.

Example of Establishing a Process of Accountability

This is example comes from a warehouse environment from which food is distributed and delivered to restaurants. The following accountability plan was established in a warehouse team meeting with all handlers and team leads present.

Set the expectation: To follow freshness guidelines at all times by executing the First In, First Out inventory method within the warehouse.

Clarify: First in, first out means the last product brought in goes to the back of the line to be picked last. The first product to enter the warehouse should be placed at the front of the line to be picked first. Are there any exceptions? No. Regardless of workload or product velocity, everyone is required to follow the FIFO method at all times.

Determine how you measure results: Freshness ratings are captured weekly in a warehouse audit. Our current rating is 87% for the year. We will look at this rating weekly to ensure we are on track to increasing our total year freshness number by nine points.

When do we check-in?

At the end of each month, we will have freshness team meeting to review results and ensure we still have a solid action plan. We will discuss each individual employee's adherence to the freshness guidelines in our weekly one-on-one meetings.

Consequences/Impact

- For every point in which we increase our freshness rating, we save the company $13,000 in shrink per year.

- For every point in which we decrease our freshness rating, we cost the company $13,000 in shrink per year.

If individuals are found not to be following the FIFO method, one warning will be given. After that, we will follow the Corrective Action process as outlined in the Employee Handbook.

When we reach our goal of increasing our freshness by nine points this year, each team member will receive an award and the team will get a lunch party.

Summarize in writing: Please sign the below indicating that you understand and are committed to executing the above accountability agreement we have established as a team. Everyone's role will be essential to us reaching our goal.

Brainstorm: How can we ensure we meet our goal?

Responses:

- We need team-building activities to increase team spirit and communication
- Add an additional forklift to the warehouse floor, as one is always broken, slowing down the rotation process
- We need an additional team member rotating the warehouse on Wednesdays and Saturdays. We currently don't have enough time or people to do it as it needs to be done
- Delay the arrival of the Hanover truck by two hours on Wednesdays to give the warehouse team enough time to rotate the warehouse

RULE #12: GET THE RESPECT OF THOSE THEY RESPECT

#influence

#persuasion

#respect

#relationshipmanagement

#managingup

#teamwork

Do you remember when we talked about **PSS's** (Peers, Superiors and Subordinates) at the beginning of this book? This rule directly relates to the peer component of the PSS, which we haven't talked much about yet.

As sucky as it may be, what people think about you matters. Why? Because quite simply, people influence people. It has been that way since the beginning of mankind—yes, well before Instagram influencers were a thing—and it will always be that way.

Because that's the case, as budding leaders, we might as well figure out how to navigate influence and use it to our advantage.

I'm about to drop a bomb on you that you're probably going to hate. I know I did when I was where you are. Are you ready?

Your team members' respect for you is often determined by an aggregate of the thoughts and the amount of respect the top five influencers in their professional circle have for you. Because people influence people, your team members' initial thoughts of you will be influenced by the thoughts of those they trust—those who influence them.

These influencers can vary but I'll bet you at least two of the five are the people who have the same job as you but have been around a lot longer—your peers. These people have seen and done enough to have acquired the respect of their team members and peers. To the people you are now leading, their opinion matters a great deal. If you want the respect of your team members, you're going to have to earn it from these people first.

So, how do you gain the respect of your peers? Very similarly to the way you gain the respect of your team members. By:

- Being reliable/dependable (follow up and follow through)
- Being a team player (helping your peers out when necessary)
- Contributing in meetings in a way that adds value
- Executive presence (we'll talk about this more later in the book)
- Being humble

LOOKING GOOD

In the distribution center where I worked at F&B Company, there were about five districts run out of that particular building. The majority of the managers there were new, like me, but there were two managers who'd been around for decades and had tons of experience. Unlike those of us who came in right out of college and into a managerial training program, these folks had once been route salesmen, for years doing the job of those I now managed. Because of their experience and the fact that they'd worked their way up, those two managers had automatic respect from the route salespeople. Don't get me wrong, transitioning into suddenly leading those that were once their peers presented a unique set of challenges for them as well, but respect for their work ethic and belief in their capabilities weren't on that list.

It was impossible for me, coming in as a college graduate, never having done either of those things—run a route, or managed a team—to get the same level of respect as these two guys, Jeffrey and Steve, right off the bat. I did want it, though. I had to develop a rapport with Jeffrey and Steve, and associate myself with them in the eyes of our route people. When one of them had a question about a customer or a process that for one reason or another I was more acquainted with, I made it a point to answer that question or get them an answer. If I was on call and one of these employees ran into an obstacle, I made sure I did everything possible to fix the problem. If there were small things around the distribution center which needed to be done to benefit all of our teams, I'd do it. If there was a need for me to step up to take some of the burden off of the entire operation, not just my team, I was stepping.

For instance, I've mentioned how crazy holiday weeks were at F&B, haven't I? Well, on the major ones, we'd need to take out so many snacks that it wouldn't all fit on the everyday route trucks we used, so we'd have to rent Penske trucks to take the additional product to the stores. Sometimes Penske would deliver the trucks, and other times someone needed to go pick them up, as well as make sure they got back at the end of the week. It was a small and nuanced task, but it was important. I'd let the more experienced managers book the trucks—the easy part—and another younger manager and myself would take on scheduling and staffing of the team members needed to make the deliveries for each district and ensure the trucks got back on time. Not only did that task help out Jeff and Steve, but it showed them I could take initiative. With that comes a head nod and a deposit into our relational bank account.

Aside from that, I would do other little things, such as help them build displays, especially if it was a massive one that required extra hands, or cover their district while they were out on vacation, or help them run a route if they had a team member call out sick. And they would do the same for me. We'd built a relationship over time of support and...you got it...*respect*.

Another way I gained the respect of my peers was by taking the time to build personal (yet professional) relationships with them, hanging out after meetings, going to lunch together or sometimes going to happy hour. This enabled us to build a friendly rapport versus a business exchange. Both balanced each other out.

Lastly, I made sure I was *buttoned up* and organized, as I noticed Jeff and Steve were. If they were organized people, as was our boss, by the way, would they think I had a handle on the business if they walked into my office with a question and there were papers all over the desk, floor, chair and everywhere? Likely not. It was important for me to display that I had a handle on my processes and potentially my business.

I give you this same advice, my friend. Be organized to gain the respect of your peers.

I do realize it probably sounds like I'm telling you that you need to look good to other people, and I absolutely am. Why? Well, we've already covered the fact that people influence people, but besides that point, your team will one day complain to the people they trust, and you want peers who respect you enough to come to your defense, using their influence with your team in support of you. Because let's face it—people like to complain, and they do it a lot. As much as you'd like to be a perfectly-loved leader, you will get complaints from people on your team, and someone has to field those complaints. If you've taken the time to invest in your relationship with your peers, instead of chopping it up with the guys about what a bad leader you are, they'll be defending you. How can you tell you have earned the respect of your peers? If they are sticking up for you and/or investing in you!

ADDING VALUE

Meetings are a great place to earn respect, but it's also very easy to lose respect, as well. Let's take a quick look at ways you can gain respect in a meeting and ways you can lose it.

Before we hop in, I should preface this by saying everything I mention may not apply to your team's culture. Some meetings are more bureaucratic than others. Some cultures invite others to speak up and some do not. With that, I would say your first step should be getting a hold of the culture in the first few meetings. Simply observe the first couple of meetings. When do attendees talk? Do they wait until the presenter asks for questions or do they pose their questions whenever they arise? Do they raise their hands or do they just blurt out their thoughts? Does this behavior change across various presenters? Who is doing most of the talking from an attendee perspective? What is the body language in the room when these attendees speak? Are they adding value to the conversation? If so, how? These are all great questions to guide your observation of the first couple of meetings.

After your first meeting, you'll probably know who the more vocal team members are. During the next meeting, try sitting beside those people, or someone who has been with the company a long time. You'll learn how they speak and when they speak, and can also lean over for a side conversation much easier if needed. You can whisper questions about acronyms or company jargon you may not understand or make a comment you would consider making to the group to gauge their response.

By the third meeting, you should be able to find an appropriate way to add value to the conversation once or twice, depending on the length of the meeting. When you do decide the time is right to contribute to the meeting, speak with authority, vigor and confidence to ensure you earn respect. Start by only speaking on topics about which you have knowledge. Adding value by sharing knowledge during a meeting is a way of establishing yourself as a voice to be listened to. You can share best practices, files or resources you've found to help you in managing your team and daily responsibilities.

If you don't feel confident sharing knowledge just yet, or feel like you have no knowledge to share, ask a solid, thought-provoking question. This is a great way to make your voice heard, it doesn't require great knowledge and won't come across as cocky. It may also challenge the perspectives of the people in the room without calling anyone out directly, which can be uncomfortable to some but does provoke respect.

Lastly, you'll want to avoid doing anything to lose respect in your first meetings. Being a know-it-all or talking too much is certainly not suggested.. To your more experienced peers, you may come across cocky and quite entitled or Millennial-like. You'll quickly lose your peers' respect by speaking too much unless those comments are questions.

Another way one could lose respect during a meeting is by appearing disengaged. If you're on your phone or computer, or you are barely paying attention to the presenter—even if the person isn't your boss—you're sending a dangerous signal to your peers that you are immature and lack the ability to listen attentively for long periods at a time. You're proving the Millennial and Gen Z stereotypes right. Many people feel that if the subject matter being presented doesn't directly impact their results, they don't have to listen. This is a fallacy when it comes to your brand in the workplace—not to mention that if you follow my advice and sit beside someone talkative, they will naturally draw the room's attention in your direction and regardless of the topic, you don't want to be caught scrolling through your phone or visiting La-La Land.

RULE #13: LOSE THE FOLLOWERS

#collaboration

#teambuilding

#inclusion

#delegation

#listening

#servantleadership

"The best leaders aren't followed…they're joined."
- Raven Solomon

In the age of social media, where everyone relishes the idea of gaining more and more followers, to hear someone say *DON'T follow me* probably sounds as rare as a pig that flies!

But, I mean it…as it pertains to leadership, of course.

I personally believe true leaders create **partners**, not followers. The best leaders set the vision, lead the team toward the vision and the team, being so compelled by the leader and his or her vision, join the leader in pursuit of it. To be a leader who's joined, not followed, means that your team believes in you, your vision and their capability to contribute so strongly that they come alongside you as you run the race towards the realization of that vision, as the above image depicts.

This is not a spiritual book by any means, but honestly, one of the best examples I can think of is in the Bible. It is there I find one of the greatest servant leaders in the history of mankind: Jesus. When Jesus decided to travel and spread the message of the Gospel, he knew he couldn't do it alone, so he went looking for help. I'm not totally sure why he chose the men he did, but I noticed when he did choose them, he allowed the disciples to see his work first, buy into his mission and make the decision themselves whether or not they wanted to be a part. He gathered his disciples—his team—not by saying, "Get behind me," but by saying, "Come join me."

Later on, we read of Jesus literally washing the feet of his *followers*, those who'd come to hear him speak. Talking about humility and leading by example. From reading about the life and leadership of Jesus, I learned that if you are a servant first, you can be most effective as a leader, and that you get much farther when you invite people to come alongside your vision, rather than demanding they go after it.

When I started my career at F&B Company, I was fortunate to be able to work with someone who practiced servant leadership in real life. One of the people who hired me was a man named Travis. Travis was a Regional Vice President, and he was one of the most hands-off leaders I'd ever come across, yet was one of the most effective. He gave his team a tremendous level of autonomy. Regardless of what the company said about having mandatory checkpoints and other management norms, Travis said to us via his actions, "I trust you. I trust that if I set the vision, you will join me." Don't get me wrong. If we had a problem, we could always come to him—we knew he was there for support. He just didn't need to manage us all the time. He trusted that if we didn't get the results we were looking for one week, we'd fix the problem and get results the next week.

We did whatever Travis needed us to do, not because he was our boss, but because he trusted us to do it. He was a great example of bringing people along with you. When we would have our yearly strategy meeting to ramp up for the coming year, Travis always presented a simplified strategic plan that everyone could understand and easily get behind. We could tell he considered his team when coming up with the strategy, and I learned later he gave his direct reports some level of input when coming up with the plan. He was good at getting buy-in from the team.

To be an effect servant leader, your team has to have some say in the direction and the pace of the race. You want them to be invested in the success or failure of the vision, like Travis so seamlessly did.

Because of how I just described Travis, we didn't blindly follow him—we happily joined him in his efforts.

Team members are most effective when you make them feel more like partners than subordinates. It really is the age-old conversation about management versus leadership, in some ways. Managers give direction, telling the team where to go. Leaders show the team where to go. Your team needs to be inspired by you, respected by you and valued by you.

THE *SUPER BOWL* OF SNACKS

I was a mid-level regional manager at F&B in Charlotte, the year the Carolina Panthers made to the Super Bowl. It was only the second time the Panthers had ever made to the Super Bowl and it was a BIG deal. The last time it had happened, I was still in high school!

To add some context, as you probably already know, the Super Bowl is one of the biggest holidays for the snack industry, and if your area's team is in it, it will likely be the biggest of all. No doubt about it, local retailers will sell more chips, crackers, cookies, dips, etc. in that week than any other week of the year. For that reason, no store…and I mean no store, wants to be out of chips. The pressure is on every snack company to deliver quality service and have plenty of product. At that time, I had well over 2,000 stores I was responsible for. That's over 2,000 store managers and probably about 150 district managers all looking for their shelves to be full of chips.

That's a lot of chips!

We needed as much time as possible to plan out something like this. There are only two-weeks between the last playoff game and the Super Bowl and the lead time on a truck load of chips was at least four weeks. So as the leader, I needed to make a decision. However, I knew I couldn't make it alone. If the Panthers didn't make it to the Super Bowl, we would all have to get rid of truckloads of extra chips. Not an easy thing to do. Therefore, I needed everyone's buy-in. We would assume the risk together.

I held a meeting with my right-hand person and my operations manager. We sat down for about an hour-and-a-half and whiteboarded all of our locations, how much extra product we might potentially need, how much we could possibly get, and how we would house all of the extra product. (Our facilities were only so big.) Lastly, we assessed the risks and detailed an exit strategy should it be needed. We looked around the mini table in my office, shook our heads and said, "Let's do it." The next thing you know, we were planning to have trailer-loads of chips brought in from all of the east coast to Charlotte, betting that the Panthers would win.

Now, it was time for me to plan the execution component of our plan. Securing the product is one thing. How we get it in the stores is a completely different challenge. Just like with the supply-chain planning, I knew I couldn't plan this level of execution on my own. I needed the brain power and experience of every leader on my team in order to pull this off. We also needed every manager and route person bought in, in line and ready to run when the time came.

I called another meeting—this time, with my right-hand person and all of my district leaders.

I told them we'd decided to pull the trigger and bet on the Panthers going to the Super Bowl. They acknowledged their alignment. I told them of our plans to get them extra product. They understood. I then told them that together we needed to plan how we'd execute. I gave them my thoughts on a plan, and for about an hour they ran with it and devised a strategy. It was intricate, it was expensive and it would require everyone putting up chips on Super Bowl Sunday—including me.

We shared the vision with our route sales people and most, if not all, got behind the plan. I put the money and resources behind it and we executed - *Flawlessly*.

I asked my team to join me versus follow me and we KILLED Super Bowl in Charlotte together.

The result? Not only did we run the highest numbers we'd run all year, but not one store out of over 2,000 called to complain that there weren't enough chips on their shelves. Not one single customer call. That is abnormal even for a regular Sunday. By giving my team a voice in the planning process and executing **our** plan together, we got the job done *right*.

I understand not every week is going to be the Super Bowl, however. So, how does one lose followers and create partners on a day-to-day level?

CREATE A CULTURE OF INCLUSIVITY

Inclusivity starts from the way you listen to the way you speak. Believe it or not, the way you phrase your language can absolutely have an impact on whether the people you lead feel included or excluded. You can say the same thing two different ways—one makes your team members feel like they're playing the game and the other makes them feel like they're just spectators. One way makes them feel like they play a role in the results and the other like they simply observe.

Here is an extremely practical example. Make it an intention to use the terms *we* and *us* instead of *I* and *me*, when talking about the business. When talking to your team members, replace *You need to* with *We should*.

Example:

"I have to hold you accountable for your actions."

"We have to hold you accountable for your actions."

"You need to fix you sales numbers."

"We should figure out how we can improve your sales numbers."

Something that small can make your team feel included versus excluded. Let's take a look at some larger things you can do to create a culture of inclusivity in your work group.

Permit

Allow Team Members to Contribute to the Construction of the Vision

As mentioned in my Super Bowl of Snacks story and my discussion of Travis' leadership, it is important to give your team members space to contribute to the team's vision-setting. What do they believe the team mission to be? What do they envision for the team this year and how do their personal goals play into that? What do they believe it takes for the team to win this year? And so forth and so on. Allowing your team to contribute increases buy-in, but it also gives them ownership as partners.

One way to ensure you team members have the ability to contribute to the vision is to establish leadership roles or subject matter expert roles within the team. Allow each member to lead in some way to increase their ownership and capacity to contribute. Not everyone feels comfortable or has the educational background to feel confident contributing in that way, so I wouldn't push. But for those who desire to progress in their careers and express that desire, this can be a great win-win. Some people are worker bees, and that's okay. You should still hold them accountable and get the best out of them from a contribution standpoint. Perhaps they contribute more to the execution.

Delegate

Let Go of the Reins Sometimes and Give Up some of the Heavy Responsibility

Give away a little power, gain a lot progress. I know it can be scary, especially when there is a lot of pressure and expectations put on you from above. But the risk of not doing so is far greater than the benefits received. If you don't delegate, you will end up with a team who is simply marching to the cadence you're screaming out. There's no real progress, because the team can only go as far as you take them. You're just one person. Give them and yourself the gift of empowerment.

Listen

Always Provide Opportunities for Feedback—and afterwards, Follow Up and Follow Through

Feedback happens constantly and it is not always verbal. You are not always listening for an audible voice. Sometimes you'll get feedback from someone's body language, so it's important to listen non-audibly, as well (We will talk more about body language in a later chapter). To create a culture of inclusivity, be aware of the feedback your team is giving you. Pay attention during your meetings. Are people disengaged, slouching in their chairs? Or are they fully-engaged, listening and contributing? Do they feel comfortable in voicing their concerns to you? They should. One sure sign of whether you have an exclusive culture or an inclusive culture, followers or joiners, is if you are getting pushback from your team. If you never receive any pushback from your team, it's not because your leadership and ideas are perfect. It is likely because they don't feel comfortable telling you how they really feel.

Update

Constantly Keep the Team Abreast of any Progress toward the Vision, creating Excitement and Increasing Continual Engagement

Let's say I tell how great a book is, get you all excited about the plot and suddenly stop at Chapter 8. You'd be disappointed, right? You'd think about it for a little while and then you'd leave and never come back to it. If the topic came back around, you'd probably be a lot less excited and likely wouldn't buy-in.

Your team is no different when it comes to getting updates on the progress toward a vision they played a role in setting. Inform them regularly of the progress so they feel like they're still walking on the path with you. Otherwise, they may feel like they're just watching.

When is a good time to update people? It depends on what the goal is. When it came to the Super Bowl situation, it was important for me to update my team daily on our progress towards the goals and strategies we were using, because it was that big of a task. But for more routine visions for year-long goals, I would suggest breaking it into quarters at least and using optional touchpoints to update them on any bigger news items in between.

If there is nothing else you take away from this chapter, I want it to be that the worst types of leaders are ones who bark commands, who don't give a voice to the people under their influence, who aren't open to feedback and who don't relinquish control to those they lead. There is no compromise in this type of leadership, nor is there much promise. Sure, you can absolutely accomplish something using fear as your leadership tactic, but over time, the respect your team has for you as a leader will dwindle and your results will be short-lived. You may score the points, but your retention may suck. As a leader, it's important to understand how important making a mark on the business is, as opposed to positively impacting the people you lead. You're always going to have some followers at various points, but your goal should be to convert those followers into joiners whenever possible.

RULE #14: PUT DOWN THE PHONE

#courtesy

#respect

#mindfulness

#executivepresence

#listening

#bodylanguage

This one, my friend, is quite simple. It doesn't require strategy, it doesn't require much thought. It simply requires discipline. Are you ready?

Put...down...the...phone.

That's it. In meetings, around the office, working with your team, during lunch—make it a point to put down the phone and engage!

I don't know about you, but I hate seeing two people at a dinner table or on a park bench and both of them are on their phones. It just reminds me of how much time we are wasting in enjoying special and memorable moments with those we love. In fact, the next family or friend function I have, I'm putting a small basket at the door and strongly encouraging all guests to drop their phone in it! In our personal lives it matters and it matters in our business lives even more.

As young leaders, the reality is we already have a reputation of being tech-dependent, and not being able to survive a single moment without our cell phones. When we are glued to our devices in a business environment we are proving correct this notion and sending a message of immaturity. It can even come across as disrespectful in some cases, even if it wasn't meant that way. For you, as a Millennial or Centennial, it probably doesn't equal that, but for someone of an older generation, it most certainly can. But you have to think about how your use of technology is being interpreted by other generations.

In November of 2018, electronics insurer Asurion completed a study that found that the average American checks their phone every 12 minutes, or about 80 times per day.[1] Many respondents struggled to go just 10 minutes without looking at their phone, Asurion researchers said. According to a survey by Qualtrics and Accel, millennials check their phones even more often: 150 times per day on average.[2]

In Rule #3, we talked a lot about the generational difference as it relates to technology and communication. You and I grew up, for the most part, with cell phones and even smartphones. Baby Boomers and many Xers, on the other hand, did not. They are far less addicted to their phones than we are and favor other types of communication, such as face-to-face dialogue and written emails. If in the middle of a communicative form they value, they see you stop to answer a text message, that could easily come off as disrespectful and disregarding of the connection they are trying to make. When you don't engage them you run the risk of them disengaging. And just like any relationship, once someone disengages because they've been offended, it can be hard to recover.

So, who exactly might you offend by being on the phone too much?

It's not just your direct reports around whom you want to avoid being stuck to your phone. Anyone you come in regular contact with during your work—team members, customers, superiors, peers—might be turned off or offended if they see you constantly on your phone. Your superiors will be the first to confront you, however. If your boss is good, they'll let you know this is an area in which you need to mature. On the contrary, if you've offended someone you are managing on your team, they might be afraid to confront you directly. As we mentioned in the prior chapter, they may shut down and simply become silent followers, which is something we want to avoid. This can be particularly diminishing to your personal brand over time simply because you won't get the chance to correct the situation or address the issue.

But what if nobody sees me
when I'm on the phone, Raven?

I'll tell you the truth, my friend. If you feel like you're not being watched all the time, then you haven't been paying close attention as you've read this book. If you remember nothing else from this chapter, it should be that you are indeed being watched. If it's not by your team, it's your superiors, and if not them, it's your peers. And not them, then someone around the office. Someone will always be there to note if you're doing what they believe to be right or not. You want to give them the least amount of issues about which to talk.

Why does it matter what other people see and think? In order to formulate a well-rounded opinion of you, your supervisors and their supervisors will often go to other people to get the information they need—especially if the organization is large. They'll literally ask a few people, "*What do you think about so and so?*" And then they'll form an opinion of you based on that information. People do this all the time. And these opinions are often solicited for important decisions like promotions. People don't think of it that way, but everyone has a circle of influence and a touchpoint with management, and those circles overlap in ways that would surprise you. So, if you think nobody who *matters* is going to see you playing on your phone, that's absolutely not true.

SET BOUNDARIES

In the case of spending time with your team, you may be thinking—well, what if it's not for personal use, but for business? Can't I use the phone then?

It's understandable as a manager that even if you're out with employees spending the day with them, your world doesn't stop. You still have a full-time job happening in real-time, even as you are helping others to do theirs. So is it wrong for you to want to get some work done during that time? Of course not. I would simply encourage you to be upfront and honest with your team member beforehand and to set boundaries.

I'll be honest—I learned this one the hard way.

There were times I'd be out working with my team members and my phone was constantly ringing. Not only was I guilty of not shutting it off, I was guilty of actually taking business calls I knew could wait. If I'm truthful, I think part of me wanted them to see how busy I was to help them understand I work hard and that when I miss their call, this is probably why. However, what I should have done is set better boundaries so I could dedicate my attention to their needs.

Of course, you can't deflect every call and every question, but you also can't be everything to everybody. You must strike a balance between being accessible and yet attentive to the people standing in front of you. I know that is easier said than done, especially when you're new, because you're trying to prove yourself and you feel like you have to be everything to everybody. I want to assure you, however, that your team will actually respect you more when you have logical boundaries which you stick to. Over time, I am confident you will become more comfortable saying *no* and establishing boundaries which allow you to give people your undivided attention.

So what does setting boundaries so you can give those you're working with, or the work you're working on, your full attention, actually look like?

Set expectations- Let the party you are working with know how long you plan to be with them and what your intentions are. For instance, if you plan to be with them until the start of your next client meeting at 2 p.m., let them know you intend to do one email check in the middle of that time to ensure there are no fires requiring your immediate attention.

Communicate your plans- If you know you are expecting two calls around lunch time or an important email from your boss, communicating that at the top of the day brings your team into the loop, tells them what to expect and eliminates any feelings of neglect during that time.

Your team knows you still have a business to run. But they also want and need their time with you—especially your Baby Boomers and Millennials—and they appreciate common courtesy and communication. You can't go wrong setting the expectations and communicating the plan, as it helps you manage their expectations.

PRACTICING DISCONNECTING

I know it's hard to wean yourself off your phone and we all struggle with it. Let's look at a few practical techniques I've found helpful.

Turn off sound notifications

Turn off your sound notifications at work so your phone is not constantly buzzing or beeping, tempting you to look at it every two seconds. Just like many folks do at night, set *do not disturb* hours on your device for your work hours.

If you're business is like mine was and is today, you still need to check your cell phone and often use it to do business. One tactic I've found helpful in not only managing my brand but also helping me be more productive is:

Set a timer for every 30 minutes or so to check your phone

Instead of being disturbed every two seconds by notifications, your phone or computer only goes off every 30 minutes, alerting you to check your phone. It saves you time and allows you to focus much better for longer increments of time. You can still stay on top of the things you need to, knowing there will be a maximum 30-minute delay in getting back to someone.

If you're worried about missing very important emergencies on the personal end, use the setting on your phone which allows certain contacts to bypass your *do not disturb*.

In meetings, turn your phone to off or silent

If you're in a meeting, definitely set your phone to silent, *do not disturb* or turn it off entirely. As I mentioned earlier, meetings are proving grounds for your leadership and you want to be found engaged, attentive and mature.

Download social media time management app

There are apps out there that track your time on the social media apps and makes them inaccessible past a daily limit you set. There are also apps that block use of social media apps during a certain time block set by you. To help curve your phone addiction during work, maybe you block yourself from using Instagram between the hours of 8 a.m. and 6 p.m.?

Technology and phones are not all bad. They are important communication tools we use to do business. Just like anything, though, we have to manage it to ensure we are using it at the right times, for the right reasons and in the right ways. In Rule #3, we talked about Communicating Their Way. If your team and the office around you, including your boss, is mostly Millennial, your cell phone usage may be seen differently. However, given that this book is about navigating multigenerational offices, I would suggest adhering to the above advice and putting…down…the phone. Take control of your phone usage and set parameters. Otherwise, it'll be in control of you.

RULE #15: PASS THE CREDIT

#humility

#delegation

#motivation

I personally believe one of the most mature and leadership-like things someone can do is credit their team and others around them for their successes. Not all leaders do this, but the more seasoned and senior leaders do; the ones with the most executive presence. My assumption is you want to be one of those leaders.

If I had to credit anything for my accelerated path, it was mimicking what I saw. I watched the people who were most impressive, the ones I most respected, and I learned from their behavior. How they spoke, how they walked, how they handled tough situations, and so on. One thing I noticed in observing these people is they rarely ever took the credit for their successes. They always passed it off, but in a very confident way.

Whether you've noticed it or not, you've probably seen this done hundreds of times. Star athletes after hitting the game-winning shot, billboard-chart topping pop artists after winning a Grammy, politicians after winning an election. Most of the time, they thank their team members, mentors and everyone under the sun. Rarely do they take all the credit. Some of them realize it took far more to get them there than their own skills and abilities and others are just saying what they were taught.

That's right—passing the credit doesn't always come naturally. Professional athletes, politicians and even executives are often trained by public relations professionals, speech coaches, brand managers, etc. on saying the right things the right way. Conveying the right message to their audience and/or the public eye is important because they want to ensure it aligns with their overall brand messages and paints them in the best, most well-received light. The same applies to you as a leader. You want the things you say and the messages you convey to demonstrate strong, mature leadership qualities.

As we all know, there are plenty of successful people who do the opposite and take credit for everything. To that, I would simply encourage you to think about the type of leader you want to be and the legacy you want to leave behind. If you were to be this type of leader, your team may interpret the message that you don't appreciate their hard work, that you're selfish and willing to undermine their contributions to hog all of the credit for yourself. I'd wonder what your true motives were. There's no worse feeling than to put in all the hard work and have someone else swoop in and take the praise. As a servant leader, particularly, it is fitting for you to share the credit.

On the other hand, to your partners, peers, customers, etc. (those around your job), taking the credit for everything sends a message of insecurity and arrogance. Very few people want to work with arrogant pricks who take the credit, especially for the deeds they didn't do. It is immature and not reflective of a quality, well-rounded leader.

The simplest way to put it is when you make your people feel like superstars, that makes you a superstar.

When you acknowledge your people, it boosts your team's confidence, makes them feel proud, and increases morale. You may think it's just a job for which they are rewarded with pay and that should be satisfactory. However, for most, job satisfaction is far more than getting paid—it's also being acknowledged and appreciated for your work.

When you acknowledge the work of your team by passing the credit, it makes them even more willing to succeed. Because, naturally, they want that praise and positive attention again.

PRAISE IN PUBLIC

So, when is a good time to pass the credit? You can do it one-on-one or behind closed doors, but it's important to pass the credit to your people in public spaces—in front of other team members and especially among supervisors and higher-ups.

At F&B Company, we had what we called market tours, where senior executives flew in from headquarters and toured the local stores in our specific area. Of course, during these times we went above and beyond to demonstrate all we were capable of doing from an execution and sales standpoint. We'd find a tight pocket of five or so stores where, as a company, we had good relationships and make a quick route. As a district manager of any given store on the route, which I was at the time, I wasn't in the store every day. So it really wasn't my relationship we were leveraging for these types of "dog-and-pony shows." We were really leveraging the route salesperson's relationship and service standards to that store. At the end of the day, it was their good work, their products, and their relationships that were about to make me look good or bad.

During one of these market tours, we stopped at a Walmart in my district. We had to have thirty different displays in that store. It was a ridiculous amount of product. I recall walking the store with the senior executives, about 10 of them, when suddenly, my boss's-boss's-boss stops, looks me dead in the eyes and says, "This is the best Walmart I've ever seen."

My insides jumped! We'd worked all day and night on this store for the past week. I could have replied, "You know, I planned this and I did that and I, I, I..." After all, it's not everyday you get to put your foot forward in front of your boss's-boss's-boss, so I wanted to make sure it was the best. Instead of pushing myself forward, however, I referred to the route salesperson and said, "John really has a phenomenal relationship with the store, providing them top-notch service day-in and day-out. He is one of best." My salesman was standing right there—and so were his bosses for about five levels. He relished it. Although he wasn't much one emotion, I could tell it was the highlight of his week. And to add the icing to the cake, it made me look like a rock star, too, because it showed my maturity and what I later knew to call *executive presence*.

TAKE CREDIT FOR THE RIGHT THINGS

It is important for me to note that I'm not talking about passing credit in a way that comes across as a lack of confidence. Women, especially, can be seen as being too humble sometimes, so I don't want you to think you shouldn't take any credit at all. I simply want you to take credit for the right things. I want you to pass the credit for the success of the accomplishments to your team, while you take the credit for leading them there.

A good example is a film or music producer. They hear something in their heads or see a finished product, but it becomes their job to find the right talent, communicate what they see effectively to that talent and coach that talent until they all reach a point where each of their contributions create the whole of the vision and/or sound the producer had in mind. There is a drummer, a violinist, a songwriter, a pianist and so many others who play a role. Leadership in the business sense is the same way. Each of your team members has a role to play in the achievement of the overall vision. Making sure everyone understands their role, executes accordingly and is coached to peak performance is your job. And when that happens, they get the credit for the song. You get the credit for producing it.

You don't do your team's job for them, do you? So why would you take the credit for their accomplishments when they do? You are there to grow them, coach them and accelerate their development— and that is exactly what you need to take credit for. When you are being reviewed by your supervisors, take credit for leading your team. Do tell your bosses how you coached your team members to this point. Reference how you closed the capability gap they had, if any. How you created processes and structure and brought certain team members together to bring the team a desired level of success. Show how you got them from Point A to Point B and how you leveraged everyone's strengths and created a harmonious environment that drove the team forward.

The most mature and poised leaders don't take the praise or the credit for the success of something which took a multitude to achieve. They give the team credit for the success and take the credit for leading the team and potentially pulling the best out of the unit. The next time you watch the star quarterback of the Super Bowl team give his speech on the field or an actress make her acceptance speech for an Emmy, notice how they effectively and skillfully pass the credit.

PART THREE:

AROUND THE JOB

Rules for Leading Effectively
Outside of Your Team

RULE #16: MAKE IT CLEAN OR MAKE IT PRIVATE

#discipline

#businessetiquette

#personalbranding

Based on the title of this chapter, you probably have some idea to what I'm referring already. Yes, I am referring to your beloved social media accounts. This chapter is all about social media etiquette.

Remember, one of your most prevalent goals as a new leader is to earn and maintain respect. In order to do that, you have to be seen as *respectable*—one whose leadership and presence warrants respect. Let me say, a half-naked selfie or live coverage of last weekend's beer pong tournament doesn't exactly do that from a professional standpoint.

Now that you are a professional and leader, and honestly even before then, you have to censor yourself online the same way the company you work for has to censor itself. Unfortunately, the days of you posting whatever you want to post or saying whatever you want to say on social media—in the public domain—are over. That may be harsh or hard to swallow, my friend, but it is a part of growth.

Before we go any further, let me address one more thing you're probably thinking. Isn't censoring myself being disingenuous or phony? Nope, I would call it being mature. Do you remember our very first rule? Don't bring your whole self to work. Secondly, consider cleaning up or privatizing your social media accounts as similar to setting guardrails around your life. The presence of guardrails doesn't mean what's on the other side of the rail doesn't exist. It just means you take the proper precautions to monitor who is privy to what's on the other side.

CLEANING UP

To clean up your social media accounts simply means to delete or get rid of anything which may be deemed as inappropriate. Your definition of *inappropriate* may be very different than your company's definition of inappropriate, so let us err on the side of caution. If you are not going to make your personal profiles private, your social media accounts should now reflect your *organization's* definition of what is appropriate. Given that every company is different, how does one determine their definition of *appropriate*? Start with their social media presence. You'll be able to see very quickly if your company is more playful and casual (like a beer company or tech startup) or if it's pretty strict, like a financial or law firm, for instance. What they post may serve as a very loose guide to what might be appropriate versus Inappropriate for your own accounts.

You also may want to consider the target audience for your particular business or industry and let that play a role in determining the appropriateness of your own online presence. For the most part, you're going to find most brands err on the side of extreme caution. They aren't very political online and they don't use profanity or post provocative pictures. You should follow suit.

Another place to look for direction on what is appropriate and what isn't is the employee handbook. Check and see if they have a social media policy in their employee handbook or Code of Conduct, which is typically posted online. This should give you some overall understanding of the level of appropriateness and the culture of the company for which you work.

Another good way to determine whether something is appropriate or inappropriate to post is if it's covered under EEOC (Equal Employment Opportunity Commission) law. If it's offensive or discriminatory towards someone's race, color, religion, sex, sexual orientation, national origin, age or disability, I strongly suggest not posting it. Using this list as a baseline standard is a good place to start. Some will disagree, but in my experience, it's been effective.

Try to assess the values of your direct manager or boss. If the company is lax but the person you report to is super-conservative, fall in line with that person's definition of inappropriate. You don't have to ask, simply observe. After all, they are in many ways in charge of your immediate advancement within this company.

One last good barometer is before you post anything online, ask yourself: *Would I want my coworkers (or my boss!) seeing this?* This is a great checkpoint to ask yourself before hitting that *Post* button.

If you're still in doubt—don't post anything beyond a PG-13 rating.

MAKE IT PRIVATE

One simple way to avoid having to even think about all of the above is to simply make your personal social media pages private. I know not everyone is going to agree with this statement, but in my experience, it's the best thing you can do to manage your social media presence and its emergence in the workplace.

Note: I say *personal* because you might have a side hustle that requires a social media page or two. This isn't your personal page, and as long as there is no conflict of interest with your company, it can and should remain public.

The fact is, we are human, and we will make mistakes, guaranteed. You may have all the best intentions in the world, but you may still end up offending or alienating someone, whether you meant to or not. And that someone could be a team member, peer, customer, boss or someone else in the workplace.

We've all heard the horror stories of people posting things on social media and losing their jobs. These days we see it all the time. Nobody is immune to this— famous directors, TV actresses, CEOs, teachers, police officers, politicians and athletes have all lost their jobs because of an inappropriate post, misworded tweet or a comment taken out of context on social media. Today, companies are extremely unforgiving in this regard, because the public is so unforgiving of them. They aren't going to support people who do things in their private lives that don't support their public persona. And these days, they just aren't taking many chances.

Social media isn't private unless you make it so. And even then, it's debatable. for that reason, I urge you to privatize your social media accounts.

UNFRIEND

What you say or post may not reach a viral level that warrants your termination, but it could lead to offending people in your workplace, creating unwanted tension and a loss of respect and/or valuable rapport amidst important relationships in your business. For this reason, I'm a huge proponent of not adding coworkers as friends/ followers on social media platforms. To me, it's just too risky for my professional brand. I've been gone from F&B for almost three years now and I'm still a little leery of accepting friend requests from former coworkers—and especially former employees of mine. I am a fan of keeping my business and personal lives separate. I think my Gen X and Z members can understand me here!

So what happens if you agree to this and you get a friend request from a coworker or customer? What do you do? My personal suggestion is to be upfront about it and not add them. It keeps the waters clear, keeps you honest and your integrity intact and is an all-around safe move.

But if you do decide to add them, or it's too late and you already have coworkers on your social media accounts, I suggest you go into your privacy settings and restrict what they can and cannot see or do on your page. I know on Facebook you can set it so people cannot see certain posts or activities or tag you in posts or photos without your consent and approval. This, I believe, is a smart move to remedy what's already been done.

Here's another controversial piece of advice—don't hang out with your coworkers outside of work, unless it is a company related function like happy hour or something of the like. If you do, avoid pictures, my friend. Let's say you may have your social media accounts locked down and secure, but one of your coworkers doesn't? They take a risky picture and before you know it, you're now associated with a crazy night out on the town.

Don't get me wrong. You should definitely socialize with your coworkers, boss, etc. and go to events. Being social is part of networking with people and managing your brand. These days, you have to be social in order to climb the corporate ladder. I get it. And I was definitely social. I just did it within the confines of work—at our large meetings, at dinner after meetings, at company-sponsored happy hours, etc. I think socializing in the sandbox is completely possible and safe. I'm simply not keen on spending time together outside of it. Note that this is my opinion and simply what has worked for me. Every company culture is different, with some being more laid back than others, where people drinking together and hanging out together is the norm. I'm not as familiar with that world with the corporate background I've had, outside of the company I am personally building—and in that one, this won't be the norm. Just know that it is okay to draw a line between your personal social life and your professional social life.

KEEP YOUR BUSINESS TO YOURSELF

While we're talking about branding and image, we should probably talk about keeping your personal business to yourself in general. PSS doesn't need to know all of the details about your relationship drama, your sister's ex-boyfriend who is now low-key stalking her or your brother's infidelity that caused him to get kicked out of the house and now he's sleeping on your couch. Part of being professional is being able to separate the personal drama and the professional world. You are there to do a job, not to be the local episode of Maury.

Have you ever heard people talk about keeping their business separate from their pleasure? This is that. Like managing your social media presence, managing the personal information floating around the office about you is part of managing your personal brand in the workplace.

I've watched people ruin their own personal brands by sharing TMI (Too Much Information). Over time they diminished their reputation by oversharing or bringing too much of their personal drama to work.

Office small talk is inevitable, so you want to be personable without oversharing your personal business. I understand it's a fine line. This is where multigenerational leadership skills come into play. As a young leader, and especially if you are single, your fun weekend plans may be a lot spicier than someone who is in their 50s and married with kids. An older married person may talk about their daughter, soccer practice and family outings. You, on the other hand, may have gone bar hopping, witnessed a bar fight and experienced a bad hangover. Not exactly the same G-rated story. Being emotionally intelligent enough to discern those lifestyle differences that come with age and controlling what you share is important. Draw clear boundaries about what you share with others and what you keep to yourself. For example, maybe you resolve to not discuss your dating life at work. You don't want to talk about dating a different person every week, so you chose to not bring it up at all. Solid choice. And regardless of the conversation over Monday's lunch, you don't mention your three dates over the weekend.

Ideally, you want to project a mature, respectable and respectful image in your professional life. Establishing clear boundaries online and offline, being upfront about where you draw the line and actually sticking to it will be key to effectively managing your brand around the office.

Refrain from oversharing and becoming too familiar in your professional relationships. At the end of it all, if you respect yourself, respect others and act appropriately, others will follow suit.

RULE #17: DEMONSTRATE PRESENCE

#executivepresence
#selfconfidence
#nonverbalcommunication
#verbalcommunication
#emotionalintelligence

Have you ever heard the term *executive presence*? I hope so because we've mentioned it several times in this book already. Let me jog your memory on what executive presence is and delve deeper into the topic.

Executive presence is pretty much the corporate term for *swag*. It's your ability to take command of a room, exude confidence and stand with poise and composure, gaining both attention and respect. When you step into the room, all eyes are on you. There's also a verbal component to executive presence. It's your ability to deliver a message with conviction, connection, and charisma. It is to be influential.

Let us note that executive presence is not arrogance. It's confidence. An almost tangible confidence. In fact, the opposite of true executive presence can actually be arrogance. It can also be someone who is completely shut down, stone-faced and shows no emotion. These are leaders who intimidate with their presence. They deter you with their demeanor. They evoke fear. On the contrary, someone with executive presence *invites* with their demeanor. They draw all the attention in the room, but they also make you feel safe, welcomed and like you matter—that it's not all about them.

IDENTIFYING EXECUTIVE PRESENCE

I'd like you to imagine meeting an older gentleman with silver hair and a charming smile. He's wearing a tailored suit, with a dress shirt, no tie. He has a firm handshake, but he's personable. He looks you square in the eye when speaking to you and he doesn't forget a name. He speaks with confidence and intelligence and doesn't miss a beat in conversation. For a second, you feel like you're the only person in the room. That is executive presence.

I could have been describing any politician, for instance, Former President Barack Obama or Former Vice President Joe Biden. They have what people call the *it* factor, and in the business world, what we call executive presence. These types of people can walk into a room and without knowing who they are, people automatically think, *She's someone important.* Michelle Obama has it, Duchess Meghan Markle has it and so does Oprah Winfrey. They may be a powerful CEO, a celebrity or someone's wife, but the one thing they all carry is authority.

When these people walk into a room, we tend to look at them. Sometimes we can't keep our eyes off them. But instead of allowing their gravitational pull to overwhelm the room, they will often divert attention, and they do it well. For instance, you'll never see politicians stand in one spot. They are up walking around and working the room. This simple act demonstrates leadership and humility. After all, they are servants of the people. Princess Diana, I've heard, albeit unheard of, would go down into crowds and shake the hands of the people. She was the first Princess to do that and it made her one of the most adored princesses, and certainly the most memorable.

Not many of the people I've named, particularly those in office, were just born with this presence. Many of them trained in this art. It's carefully cultivated by professionals, just like the passing of credit skill we discussed earlier. It is practiced and practiced until it becomes second nature and comes off as their natural personalities. Unlike these remarkable public figures, most of us aren't going to hire a coach to teach us these things, but once you reach a certain level in an organization, sometimes the company will provide one for you. That may be you someday! Until then, you have to find people with executive presence and simply mimic what they do. I've learned many things about presence simply from observing others. I'm going to share four ways I demonstrate executive presence now and in my corporate career. I'm also going to give you a very practical step you can start today for each.

DEMONSTRATING EXECUTIVE PRESENCE

1. Make what you say count. Said differently, make sure what you say *adds value*.

People with executive presence don't always have the loudest voices in the room. Instead of over-talking, they read the room and they listen. They listen for the best time to contribute, and when they do, it is meaningful with lots of added value. They are polished, poised and they speak with authority—succinctly and purposefully. They don't talk just for the sake of talking. That's where you lose credibility and people start feeling like you are wasting their time.

As a young leader, you may not always feel like what you have to say is valuable to rooms full of experience. Refer back to Rule #12. Sometimes you have to assert yourself, but when you do, make what you say count.

Practical Step: Think before you speak, and when you think, try to organize your thoughts in bullet points. Thinking in an organized manner will make your delivery concise.

2. Perfect HOW you say things.

What you say matters, as mentioned above, but *how* you say it matters just as much and, in some cases, even more. When you speak, you want to speak with conviction and professionalism. You want people to take you seriously and you also want them to be able to follow along easily. Eliminate filler words such as *um*, *like*, *so* and *you know*. You'll also want to shy away from using slang like *lit*, *dope*, *drip*, *yaas*, and others.

Err on the side of caution with swear words. I didn't use curse words in front of superiors and definitely not with my team members. I've known people who do, and most of them haven't progressed in their careers. It's not appropriate, and it doesn't demonstrate presence. Think about it. When was the last time you heard your boss's boss say a cuss word in the office? It may be acceptable, but it's still unprofessional.

Practical Step: Join a Toastmasters group to practice your public speaking skills with other professionals. It is super affordable and a wise investment in yourself.

If you can't join Toastmasters, watch and learn from news anchors on TV or talk-show hosts. They use certain voice inflections and speak slower to emphasize certain points. These are the most accessible and polished examples of public speakers from whom you can learn easily and immediately.

3. Control your emotions and influence others' emotions.

How familiar are you with *emotional intelligence*? It is really the part of your brain/ intelligence most used to lead people. In short, emotional intelligence (EQ) has four parts: self-awareness, social awareness, self-management and relationship management. How aware we are of ourselves and our own emotions impacts how we manage ourselves and our relationships with others. Our own self-awareness also impacts how aware we are of others and their emotions, thus impacting our relationships with others, as well.

Figure 17.1[1]

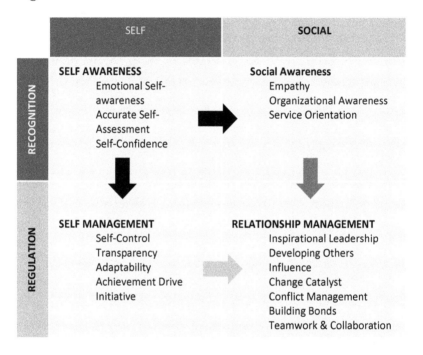

This idea of controlling your emotions and positively impacting the emotions of others falls into all four parts of emotional intelligence. The truth is, your team will constantly look to you to dictate how they should feel, especially during a major change or during a crisis situation. Part of executive presence is exuding a certain coolness, poise and control in tough situations. Those around you will pick up on that and adapt accordingly. When people are uncomfortable and there's anxiety or fear present, the best leaders rise to the top.

I found myself in this position frequently at F&B. Every year the company would enact changes which especially impacted the route salespeople who relied on commissions from their sales. The changes usually positively impacted some and negatively impacted others in the short-term. In the moments leading up to these sorts of changes, there was a lot of push back, stress, angst, fear, anger and complaints. *Emotions.* As a leader, young or old, I had to manage these varying feelings of the people I led. I had to control my own feelings, regardless of what they were, provide calm solutions and a safe place for the members of my team to vent and assure them all would be well.

You're not in control of what gets passed down to you from upper management, but you are in control of the emotions you display, and thus you have the power to influence how people feel about it. You have the opportunity to demonstrate executive presence. This works both ways for managing negative emotions and amplifying positive ones. For instance, if you're really passionate about something you impart that feeling on others. Emotions are contagious and can be effective leadership tools, as long as we control them.

Familiarize yourself with the concept of emotional intelligence to bring more attention to your emotions and how they play a part in your overall presence.

Practical Step: Read a book on emotional intelligence. I highly suggest starting with *Emotional Intelligence: Why It Can Matter More Than IQ* by Daniel Goleman.

4. Look the part (dress and posture).

When you step into a room you want people to immediately recognize you are a professional—that you're competent, direct and ready. This, in part, calls for dressing well and having good posture.

One of my good friends from F&B was a man with the worst posture—and he wasn't a very good dresser, either. However, he was super bright and was capable of one day running F&B. Seriously.

He was about one level higher in seniority than I, and I remember him getting promoted to his first executive-level job. Relevant side note: I used to be a men's stylist.

Once I learned of his promotion, I sent him a friendly email congratulating him on the job and offered to style him for free. I told him, "You're at a whole new level now. You've got to step up your game!" Unfortunately, he didn't take me up on it. He continued to dress the way he wanted and felt most comfortable. I don't think his appearance made a huge impact on his team members, but the senior leadership definitely noticed it. Eventually, he got promoted again to an even higher position, and this time they gave him some feedback. They told him, "You slouch too much. It comes off sloppy and unprofessional." He came back and told me I should include advice about this into my coaching—and that's exactly what I did and exactly why it's in this book!

Good posture and the way we dress matters, especially for demonstrating executive presence. It may not matter if you're in computer programming in a dark room all day, but once you become a leader, these things matter very much.

In Rule #7, I spoke about having a firm handshake, making eye contact, and the importance of conveying confidence in your posture. Slouching makes you look anti-social and insecure. If you're slumped over at your desk, people get a *subordinate* vibe when they approach you. Sitting and standing with your chest up and shoulders square, gives off confidence and a *leadership* vibe— and that's what you're looking to portray. If you need an example, examine the way ballet dancers stand. You should feel like you have an invisible string pulling your chest upwards. Your neck is long and your diaphragm relaxed.

Lastly, looking nice matters. My mother used to remind me that I should, *"Dress for the job you want, not the job you have."* If you want the VP Level job, dress like a VP.

Practical Step: Find the person who has the job you want and duplicate their look. Mature your dress and posture.

How? What if you don't have style? Go out and buy one fashion magazine— GQ if you're a man or Vogue if you're a woman, for instance—and find three looks that you like. Rip them out, go to nearest Dillard's, Macy's or Banana Republic and go up to a salesperson and ask,—"Can you help me look like this?" That's their job, and they are likely into style.

If you're not comfortable approaching a salesperson, look at the mannequins around the store for inspiration. The brand often has professional stylists who work at the headquarters whose job it is to create nice looks and send them to the stores for mannequin dressing.

If you're reading this book, you either already have enough money to go to the store and buy three professional outfits or you soon will. These will carry you through the next couple of years.

Getting clothes that fit also makes a difference. Clothes that fit send a message of organization, competence, confidence and more. If you don't want to spend a lot of money, you can find professional outfits from Ross or other discount stores, but be sure they fit. You can buy a $100 suit, take it to the tailor and it will end up looking like a $1,000 suit when it's done. Women, especially, make the mistake of buying work clothes that are too big for us because we want to avoid tight or revealing clothing. Baggy clothes look sloppy, and tight clothes look cheap. Get clothes that fit and flatter your body type. You can also Google examples.

I know every company has a different dress code and start-up culture is way more casual and lax, but being neat and wearing fitted clothes still goes a long way. Casual is fine, but don't wear a t-shirt with holes in it or inappropriate language on it—go to J-Crew and get a nice t-shirt.

If I haven't already sold you on the importance of executive presence, let me leave you with one quick stat. Gartner conducted a study in which they surveyed a bunch of CIOs (Chief Information Officers)—arguably the most technical function of the business. They asked those CIOs—*what are the top 20 leadership traits that make the most difference?* Number two on the list? *Executive presence.* To give context, technological skills (the technical skills of this industry) was listed as number 12. No matter how technical a field you're in, leadership requires executive presence. Start practicing this now.

RULE #18: LIMIT TWO

#professionalism
#businessetiquette
#selfawareness
#selfmanagement
#personalbranding

This chapter is about what might be an exciting topic for some and an unnecessary topic for others—*alcohol*. Even if you don't partake in alcohol, I'd suggest reading this brief chapter about it because you may need to coach an employee about this at some point.

Alcohol will likely be part of many professional functions you attend. It is often a prevalent part of afterhours meetings, networking events, social outings with clients, work parties and more. Nine times out of 10 it will be at no personal expense to you (monetarily speaking) and often available for unlimited consumption. Yep, all you can drink.

But before you get too excited, let me break the news of Rule #18 to you—your limit is now two.

Don't close the book!

For any work-related or professional occasion, I charge you to limit yourself to no more than two alcoholic drinks. Whether you are a lightweight or a heavyweight…the limit is two.

You're probably asking *why*? Because alcohol often causes us to do and say things we probably wouldn't without it. The more we drink, the more we expose ourselves to doing something we may regret—something that doesn't align with our values, our brand or the messages we teach our team members.

There's a saying that goes, "A drunk man tells no tales." When we drink, we tend to say exactly what we want to say without a filter. Any professional filter through which we typically process our words is gone out the window and we are no longer our professional selves. We become our whole selves—and as you know, he or she shouldn't be at work. Alcohol tends to loosen your tongue. You don't want to say something you'll regret. People may take this as your most authentic self, the most truthful version of you and will likely not forget what you say and/or do.

Depending on how long you've been out of the college drinking culture, you may have to shift your mentality around drinking. At a college party, and even at some adult parties, many people drink to get drunk. If that is you, let's shift your focus. In professional settings, regardless of how much is available and at what cost, you are not drinking to get drunk. You are there to socialize and build professional relationships. If drinks are a part of that, cool. They should not, however, be the focal point.

I've seen so many people ruin their careers making poor choices under the influence of alcohol. I've known people who really wanted to progress in their careers, and were capable of doing so, whose drunken nights preceded them. You don't want to be one of these people.

Just like peer pressure exists in grade school and college, it will exist in the professional world, too. I urge you to be on the lookout for it and to avoid it. Some companies are almost like the sorority or fraternity on campus, getting in trouble all of the time. People, even your superiors, will try to get you drunk to see how far you'll go. Many times it's a test. Will you pass or will you fail?

Portray the professional version of yourself at all times. There has to be some degree of separation between your work life and your outside life. You should conserve some portions of yourself from a work/life balance standpoint but also a brand-management standpoint. What people see becomes your brand.

Your generational knowledge comes in handy here. Think about it—your workaholic Baby Boomers probably need and welcome a stiff drink at a work event, but their tight approach to following workplace protocol and the value they place on visibility, title and recognition make them approach drinking quite conservatively. Your drunkenness in a professional setting will be judged harshly by them. Xers, on the other hand, may actually want to turn up with you. Their fun and informal approach may make them more prone to let loose at company functions, but keep in mind—they've already proven themselves. You, on the other hand, still have much to prove.

KNOW YOUR LIMITS

One time I attended a company event with an open bar, where everyone received two drink tickets. I knew I would have to get in front of the crowd at some point to deliver a speech, and of course, I wanted to make sure I could do that well. I was also very nervous, so I got a glass of wine to relax my nerves and drank it before my speech. I remember being up there speaking—very relaxed but a little sweaty. There was no way I could have had another drink and still have made sense. I knew my limits given the circumstances and skated far away from the line. Sometimes even one drink can be a disaster, so you have to know your body and your limits. If, based on experience, you know your maximum is one drink before you become obnoxious, stick to that.

Maybe, as a basic rule of thumb, act like your grandparents are there at the event with you. Not your parents—because some of us have very cool parents—but your grandparents. You would likely have a different level of restraint as you consume alcohol out of respect for them. I want you to have that same respect for yourself in professional settings like these.

Just because you have a one or two drink minimum doesn't mean you have to drink at all. You can always err on the side of caution and choose not to drink. Some people don't drink at professional events and I totally support that. Grab a Shirley Temple or a Coke on the Rocks with a spritz of apple juice and be on your merry way.

When I first started working at F&B Company, I didn't drink at all. I worked for a gentleman who absolutely loved Kentucky bourbon and that was his thing. The first time he offered me a drink, I declined and simply told him I didn't drink. He said "That's great. Would you mind telling me more?" I answered, "Sure. It's because of my faith." That was the only time I had to say that. He never asked again and always made sure I didn't feel uncomfortable around him. If you have personal standards which prohibit you from drinking, please uphold those and don't be afraid to communicate them to those who matter.

TIME WILL TELL

There is more alcohol in the staff kitchen than actual food. At company events, people are gossiping and oversharing details of their personal lives. Your coworkers sit around talking about their hangovers every morning...

What if your office culture is very unprofessional like this? Should you succumb, try to raise the standard or just *do You*?

Whenever I coach young professionals on how to appropriately navigate their corporate cultures, I tell them to find someone they are drawn to, someone they admire and respect, whether it's the boss or a mentor they've been placed with, and use that as their baseline standard. Even amidst all of the shenanigans, what does that person do or not do? How are they treated in the company? Are they respected or are they ostracized? Do they feel welcomed or do they feel shut out? Those answers may tell you if this is the right place for you and your standards. It is okay if it isn't. Find something different.

But what if there is no one I'm drawn to or respect?

Give yourself six months to a year and see if you and your standards can truly make it there or not. There is a possibility your standards may influence those around you to adopt a higher set of their own. People who respect you will respect your standards. For example, there are some people who do not curse. Out of respect for that person and their choices, many people try not to curse around them. That is an example both of support and how your standard could potentially influence a culture. On the contrary, if you find you're being ostracized, held back because of your standards or left out of certain circles that are essential to your job performance—you're in the wrong culture.

Sometimes you have to rise above the norm and set a higher standard. If that standard isn't appreciated, you move on.

RULE #19: BE BIGGER THAN YOUR BOSS

#personalaccountability

#selfmanagement

#professionalism

#managingup

#respect

This rule, similar to the last, is about standards—this time as it relates specifically to your boss and other leadership. Growing up, did your parents tell you that just because a person did something doesn't mean you could? My mom said this to us all the time about things like cursing or other adult things.

Similarly, you shouldn't always do what your boss/bosses do. For example, just because your boss drinks beer at a lunch meeting and cusses up a storm doesn't mean you can or should with the same results. Simply said, your bosses have earned their stripes. You haven't quite yet. As we mentioned in an earlier chapter, you still have a lot to prove.

Do you remember how Baby Boomers believe stripes are earned? *Time.* That's right. There are certain perks, if you will, that come with time and position, and one of those perks is setting the standard, be that high or low. When you become the boss, you will have this same privilege, or should I say responsibility, but as of right now, it belongs to someone else. It is not something to which you are entitled.

The last thing you want to do is perpetuate this reputation our generation has of being entitled, a sign of immaturity. As a young leader, your maturity will differentiate you and separate you from your peers.

So, what do I mean by the title of this rule—be bigger than your boss? I mean you should set a standard that's higher than your boss's. Going back to our prior rule, if your boss's rule is to follow a two-drink maximum, yours is one. If she cusses like a sailor to employees, you do not. People are not perfect, including our leaders, so there will always be something you can do that they do not.

One good rule of thumb is to look a level above for your standard. If you seek to be a better leader, even better than your boss's boss, you must be seen as being capable of having that role someday. From the inside looking out and from the outside looking in, *look capable.* And eventually, your senior leaders will see that.

During my third job with F&B, I had a boss who wore pants and a button-down shirt, sometimes a polo, daily. That was fine for him, but I wanted to demonstrate presence and set my standard higher than his, so I looked at the way *his* boss dressed as my example. She wore blazers daily and so did I. That became a standard for me in that role and in roles to come. Over time, blazers became my trademark. People did indeed notice me. I can't be certain of the mental association that made, but my next role was executive :-). Coincidence? Hardly.

RESPECTING SOMEONE YOU DON'T RESPECT

As you progress in your career, you are going to have to work for different types of people—and not all of them are going to be consummate professionals. Some people you will respect to the moon, while others you will wonder how they got where they are. Working with a boss you do not like or respect requires a lot of tact. Bad bosses can be demeaning, unsupportive, intimidating and intimidated, amongst many other things. They may not take too well to their subordinates outshining them and may view you as competition.

When I say be bigger than your boss, I'm not suggesting you should compete with your superiors. Even if they are the worst boss ever and you could do their job inside and out, the office still stands and their position is still higher than yours. Even if you do not respect the person, at least respect the office. There are probably many troops who are not personally fans of the President in office at any given time, but when in their presence, they still salute. They may not support the man (or woman) but they support the office.

Your boss has a very influential place in your career progression and that is not going to change. As you aim for a higher standard of behavior than your boss, remember it is not a competition with them. You are competing with yourself more than anything else. You are establishing an internal standard your boss cannot touch. They are verbally abrasive to their employees but you are not. They wear shorts to work on Fridays and you simply choose not to. There is no need to make a big announcement.

Every leader wants to be highly-regarded. Even you want to be respected as a leader, which is why the majority of this book is about gaining respect from your team. Remember, you want the same things your boss wants. So find the areas where you can give them that respect. There must be one thing...something you can respect about your boss, even if you generally disagree with his or her behavior. They may be the worst communicator in the world, but maybe they are really great at selling. If they are not good at sales, then maybe they are really good at resolving conflict. Or maybe they make people feel really welcomed. There must be something. I would like to think every boss has done at least one thing right to get where they are. Focus on what they are good at and try to glean wisdom from these aspects of them rather than the negative ones. I have found this helps me respect people even when I don't respect them. I'm not a Donald Trump fan but I can respect his boldness, if nothing else.

DEFERRED APPRECIATION

Holding yourself to a higher standard over time will earn you respect, but you may not see it right away. I call this deferred appreciation, which we have already covered a few times throughout this book so far, because some readers may not get it until after the fact. You probably will not see the value of this until five or ten years down the road.

Part of being a leader is creating a lasting impression, modeling behavior and leaving a legacy. Your team is going to model themselves after their leader—*you*. You might, then, want to model yourself after someone even higher than your boss.

RULE #20: WORRY 'BOUT YOSELF

#personalbranding
#discipline
#selfmanagement
#takingcriticism
#relationshipmanagement

The title of this chapter came to me after watching a viral video of a little girl, who could not have been any older than three, telling her parent to, "Worry 'bout yoself," as she struggled to put on her seatbelt in the back seat. *What sound advice*, I thought ☺).

I don't mean this to sound selfish when I say, "Worry 'bout yoself." What I mean is, instead of being all up in other people's business, tend to your own. Gossiping, spreading rumors, creating drama, etc. is so college, although sadly, you'll quickly learn it exists in the workplace, too, if not more so.

While office drama and gossip may keep you entertained or be a nice break from the craziness of a busy business, it will also keep you in the same position you're currently in— stuck, wondering why you can't get promoted.

I have personally found gossip brews in unproductive environments. When people don't want to do their work, or they can't find anything else to do, they gossip. People love to gossip in the break room, at the water fountain, at happy hour, at lunch, and some are even bold enough to do it at their desks. There is probably considerably more gossip happening in emails, text messages and IM's. Just little chatterboxes everywhere! But you need to focus, in spite of it. If you are a leader intent on achieving results and doing your work, you don't have time for gossip. Find and converse with those people who haven't jumped on the gossip bandwagon.

When you get bored or run out of work, I'm positive you can find something else to do, whether it's an extracurricular activity at work or working on a side hustle. It's a perfect time to display your maturity, presence and willingness to help.

What if there is a culture of drama and gossip at your place of business? How does one avoid it?

A few very practical steps include: Walk away when gossip starts. Be direct in telling the person you don't want anything to do with drama and stay busy. The best defense for gossip is to *stay busy*. Your excuse not to engage in the rumor mill is that you have work to do, as should everyone in the office!

If you are the *source of the tea* and you're already a part of the rumor mill, or you've been the one spreading drama—can you recover? Yes! Simply tell the people you gossip with that you don't care to do that anymore, or subtly ghost them. Have an excuse—work is usually a good one, to avoid gossiping. Scratch your drama itch by watching the latest season of *Love & Hip Hop* or *Jersey Shore*. Don't do it at work. I don't know any senior level executive who is a gossip queen/king. Being a gossip queen/king is not going to get you ahead in life or in business. Regardless of what you see on TV, the best leaders aren't catty, cutthroat or backstabbers. They stay out of the drama, demonstrate composure and skillfully resolve conflict.

While you're staying out of other people's business, you may want to make it easy for people to stay out of yours by not sharing your personal business at work, as we've mentioned a few times now. But I want to reiterate the point: *Keep your personal life personal.* If you focus on your job and doing the right things at work, you won't be around the office drama queens/kings for long. You will be promoted and they will likely remain where they are today.

AVOID NEGATIVE NANCY

The most dangerous, and likely the most prevalent, type of gossip is when people gossip about the company. Even if you are not doing the talking and are just listening, over time, this negativity will taint your image of the organization and drag your spirit down the drain. Entertaining that toxicity can be mentally draining, spiritually draining and harmful to your personal brand. You've got to be careful not to fall into that trap, especially being a new employee. I know you want to make friends and be social around the office, as you should. But you should also be careful and discerning about the thoughts you entertain and who you believe.

It's easy to identify Negative Nancy. Everything that comes out of her mouth is negative. These are disgruntled, unhappy employees who hate what they do and would kill to be somewhere else. There is very little ownership on their part. When something goes wrong it is always someone else's fault and never their own. When they speak about the company it's always "they" or "y'all." It's never "we." They've likely been hurt by the company in the past and are bitter as a result. These people have been passed up for every promotion they apply for and blame it on everyone else. Rarely, if ever, do they self-reflect. These people are unhappy and they want everyone else around them to be unhappy too. Misery loves company. These employees are negative evangelists of the company.

These are people you should limit your interaction with for a couple of reasons. 1) What you're allowing into your mind and heart about the organization you work for matters. Words are powerful. They impact our thoughts, feelings, mood and disposition. 2) If there's a Negative Nancy, their reputation likely proceeds them, even with the boss. You don't want to become associated with that person and wind up lumped into the same category. As the saying goes, "You are who you hang with."

It is okay to hear people out when they have legitimate concerns, but you are not a dumping ground for someone else's perpetual negativity. If someone constantly tries to draw you into badmouthing the organization, you can simply say, "Can we talk about something else?" Or if they persist, then ask them, "Okay, what do you suggest we do about that?" Such a question usually stops them in their tracks.

Also, be careful you don't become the Negative Nancy! There may be a time when your manager pulls you aside and asks you to dish the dirt about your peers. Every manager is going to want some level of insight into their team. The more informed they are, the better. This may relate to a specific circumstance, or maybe they're just trying to make an informed decision about the person in question. Either way, it's a sticky situation. You want to demonstrate that you're trustworthy and add value, but this could also be a test to see how far you'll go. I've been faced with this situation many times and I've simply declined to engage. I either say I don't know or I'll flip it into the most positive conversation possible. A rat can't be trusted, even by those to whom they are ratting.

If you are being asked for general buzz, then sure, supply away—but without disclosing names.

GROW A THICK SKIN

You know what they say—*if you're being talked about, you're being thought about.* So, what happens if you find yourself on the receiving end of the rumor mill?

If you find yourself the target of gossip, you will have to conduct yourself differently than a regular employee.

If you do choose to confront the person responsible for spreading the gossip, do it one-on-one. Do it in private, and do it in your calmest state—not when you're drunk or agitated. You don't want people to think they can get a rise out of you so easily. Ask them how they came to their conclusions, correct any misinformation they may have about you and be direct about it.

On the other hand, if you choose not to confront them, there's nothing wrong with turning the other cheek. As a leader, your job is to demonstrate certain characteristics, and letting things roll off of your shoulders is a big part of that.

RULE #21: EMAIL WITH ETIQUETTE, TEXT WITH CAUTION

#writtencommunication

#businessetiquette

#professionalism

#emotionmanagement

Every day, 205.6 billion emails are sent across the globe.[1] Today, it is our number one method of communicating in business. Despite the emergence of applications like Slack and Google Drive and the prevalence of other platforms like Skype and Instant Messengers, in most workplaces, email is still the dominant method of communication. We noted in Rule #3 that Xers love email, and based on figures, the rest of us either must, also, or we find it to be a necessary evil. Love it or hate it, email is a fast and easy and is a great way to leave a paper trail for future reference.

Which is why, amongst many other reasons, email etiquette is far more important than people think.

Lack of email etiquette is one of the most common frustrations I hear from HR and Hiring Managers about this generation of new employees. Even simple things like using spell check, having an appropriate and professional signature and using correct punctuation are being ignored. For a generation supposedly so adept at digital communication, we definitely have a lot to learn about the art of coming across as professional and adept in our emails.

If you haven't already noticed, I'm pretty much a huge copycat. The way I learned email etiquette was not in a class or through a book like this (lucky you). I learned it through mere observation and a lot of trial and error. I'm a decent writer (I hope you would agree) so I feel I've always been pretty good at communicating by email, but in the beginning, I really struggled with brevity. My emails would be paragraphs long when they really only needed to be a couple of sentences. I didn't really get a grasp on brevity until the fifth or sixth year into my career. Now, I'm a polite straight-shooter in email.

HELPFUL TIPS

From the day I entered the corporate world, I observed other people's email styles and consciously, as well as probably subconsciously, learned from them. If I saw an email which came across as rude, unprofessional or overly emotional, I'd take note and add it to my mental *What NOT to Do* list. If I saw an email that made me feel warm and fuzzy inside, was a nice length, direct, clean, crisp and professional, I added it to my *What to Do* list. I would use these as a standard with which to revise my own email style over time. Based on years of observation, refinement and feedback, I've put together a list of some common email etiquette guidelines just for you:

- Before you hit SEND, or even better, before you write the email, ask yourself: *Does this warrant an email?* Maybe there are more appropriate modes of communication such as a quick phone call, an instant message, or a peek over the cubicle, that may get it done faster or better.

- Plan your emails before you write them. Consider your audience, your intention and the best way to communicate your point.

- Never send an emotionally-charged email. Step away, take some time (as long as 24 hours), clear your head and maybe get a second opinion. Perhaps the email you're about to fire off is better suited as a conversation.

- Use spell-check. This sounds like a no-brainer because it's automatic these days, but some people fail to make the highlighted corrections.

- Be mindful of your audience. Know when to keep it short and sweet. Busy people lack time. The last thing they want is a two-page email. If you send an email to someone you know is busy, do you and them a favor and make it brief. Think about what some of their follow up questions might be in response to your email and try to answer those upfront to avoid a back and forth, requiring even more time.

- Use a greeting/salutation. Hello, Hi, Hi [insert name], Greetings, Happy Monday, etc.
- Proofread! Reread your email at least two times before sending it. Check for clarity, redundancy and errors.
  - o Ensure you're using the right name and that it's spelled correctly. This may sound small but if there's one error the recipient is sure to notice, it's the misspelling or misuse of their own name! Very recently I found myself emailing someone with two first names— you know, like Daymond John— and ended up calling her by her last name for an entire day because I didn't pay close enough attention.
- Avoid slang or pop acronyms- OMG, LOL, WYD.
- Size matters. Both font size and the size of attachments are important to consider.
  - o Your font should be between 10 and 12 points, no bigger and no smaller. Those with a hard time seeing can zoom in and those who like to read in smaller fonts can zoom out.
  - o Try to make your attachments as small as possible. Most people have mailbox sizes and a sure way to get your email deleted quickly is to clog up someone's mailbox. For large files, use file-sharing services and provide links.

- Use basic fonts. Don't use cursive fonts or Wing Ding. Calibri is the new Times New Roman. It's easier to read and a lot less formal. When in doubt, Google the top ten web-safe fonts and go with one of those!

- Font color should be black or dark grey unless you're highlighting a certain text.

- Try to respond within 24 hours (when in office). This won't always be possible, but it is a realistic goal for which to shoot.

- Don't overuse exclamation points. Use one-to-three maximum per email. Otherwise, your words may come across as pushy, too thirsty or disingenuous.

- Avoid emojis.

- Avoid all CAPS.

- If you've never sent this person email communication and vice-versa...introduce yourself. Don't assume they know who you are. However, be brief. Who you are, why it matters to them and what you want.(I told you, my brevity is getting better.)

- Don't BCC. (I'll go more into why later in the chapter.)

- Have a professional signature. Most companies have templates. If yours doesn't, use a professional signature-generator online. Many of them are free.

- Shave it down- For whatever reason, younger people tend to send longer emails. Maybe it's because we're enthusiastic or think we're coming across as more intelligent, as if the longer the email, the smarter we sound. I'm not sure. Just make it a point to shave down your emails before sending. In proofreading, try to shave off at least three sentences if you can.

YOUR SIGNATURE: IT'S NOT ALL ABOUT YOU

I can't tell you how many times I've needed to quickly pull up someone's email so I can get their phone number from their signature to call them for last minute directions, a quick status update, etc. and couldn't find it. How annoying! I have to rummage through email trails to find the first email they ever sent me in order to finally find it. And sometimes it's not there, either. The way I look at it, a signature is a dummy proof way for you to let people quickly know who you are and how to contact you. It should be like your business card—the digital version.

You signature should, therefore, include more than just your name. It should always, *always* include your contact information. Your email signature is not your opportunity to show off your personal flair. It's really not about you at all. It's about what the other person might want or need from you. What if they want to call you? Or need to mail you something? In this day and age, our attention spans are so short. Make it easy for people to find what they want and/or need.

Ideally, a professional signature at the bottom of your email should include your logo or the company's logo, your name, the name of your organization and a link to it, your title, and all your contact information, including your email address, mailing address, phone number, and a fax number (if you still have one of those in 2019). I've included my email signature below for a reference:

Raven Solomon
Keynote Speaker | Author | Millennial & Gen Z Leadership Expert

A 7400 Old Mt Holly Rd, #237, Charlotte NC 28130

M 704-266-0652 **E** info@ravensolomon.com **W** www.ravensolomon.com

A signature at the end of an email can also say a lot about who you are (or aren't) as a professional, and sadly, many people get it wrong.

If it's big, really bright and all over the place, if it's missing the important contact information or if it's too busy, long and the font is every color in the rainbow, I might think on one hand that this person is a very vibrant and bold person. But on the other hand, I might think that this person is all over the place or rambunctious. Surely someone has given them feedback about this signature—do they not take feedback well? Are they difficult to work with?

Also, it's tempting to insert a quote, a piece of scripture or a slogan into your signature, but these days, I personally refrain from doing it.

I used to have a Bible verse in my signature I thought was good and encouraging for business: *Planning puts you further ahead in the long run, hurry and scurry puts you further behind.* **Proverbs 21:5**. I wasn't hitting people over the head with my faith, but I eventually removed it simply because not everybody is Christian and I didn't want anything in my professional emails that might be alienating or offensive to others.

DON'T HIT SEND YET!

Before we finish our email etiquette lesson, here's some other important things to consider before your fire off an email. These also apply to text messages.

Know when to Take a Conversation Offline and onto the Phone

Texting is the primary mode of communication for our generation, and picking up the phone is difficult. Here's a good rule of thumb: if there's any emotion involved, don't text or email—it needs to be a phone call.

If you are uncomfortable speaking on the phone, you'll need to get comfortable as you prepare to lead in a multigenerational workplace. Verbal conversation is a skill. It's a muscle that has to be worked. Set a goal of making ten phone calls per week to really exercise this muscle. I don't care if you are just calling Foot Locker to find out if they have your size in a pair of Nikes you never intend to buy. Just call and talk to another human being you don't know simply to overcome emotion—in this case, nervousness—in conversation.

Over time, you will development internal ways of coping with emotions in verbal conversations. The next time you find yourself in an angsty situation with a coworker, that muscle memory should kick in.

Why, in emotion-filled situations, is it better to simply pick up the phone? Because written words can often be misconstrued and misinterpreted. The one thing we can't verbalize well through written communication is emotion. The last thing you want to do is fire off an email in the heat of the moment and say things you can't take back. Once someone has taken your words the wrong way, this can quickly snowball and lead to tense relationships with peers, employees, etc., low morale and decreased productivity. Just pick up the phone or schedule a face-to face-meeting. It may be a little uncomfortable at first but it's worth it.

Remember Emails, IMs, Texts and any of the Forms of Digital Communication Live Forever

Before you hit the *send* button, think to yourself—would you want this email or text message read out loud during a court hearing? Would you want your boss to see it? Would you be okay if others around the office saw it?

Written digital communication is permanent. Even when deleted, it can be found somewhere. And in the world of screenshots...a message could live forever. So unless you want your words to come back and bite you, I'd suggest keeping all the unintended audiences in mind before you hit *send*.

Keep it Brief

We've mentioned this, but I want to provide a little more color around this idea. I avoid long emails. I don't like reading them and I assume other people don't really like it, either. Having spent significant time in sales, I've learned that hopping on the phone or video chat is so much more effective than sending a long, explanatory email. I'll send a short email and then ask, "Can we talk through this proposal?"

Also, if you observe, the higher up people get in their organization, the shorter their emails tend to get. The Senior VP's emails are short, concise and straight to the point. They may be taken as rude, but there's no time for fluff.

Be Careful when CC'ing and BCC'ing People

People tend to overdo it with CC'ing. Before CC'ing, ask yourself— do they really need to see this communication? Does this make a difference to them or impact their role somehow?

In terms of BCC, I personally never use it at all unless it's a mass email and I need to protect people's email addresses. Outside of that, I don't think you should be BCC'ing anyone, especially with the intent of gossiping or being petty. When it comes to CC'ing your boss, remember—they are not mediators to every little qualm you have. They don't have time to sort out who is right and who is wrong on an angry 10 page email chain. You may think you're putting attention on someone else's faults by doing so, but you're actually just highlighting your own. If you're really having a problem with someone, talk to your boss about him or her and potentially loop in HR.

Cautionary Tale

I've seen many nightmare emails. Maybe that's why I've learned so quickly about what to avoid. Here's some examples of well-intentioned employees who ended up coming across less-than-professional in their emails.

I used to work with a young lady who wrote lengthy emails and put an exclamation point after everything. I mean *everything*. She sent these emails to customers, to me, to her bosses and to her employees.

One day, we had a sit down meeting. I printed out one of her emails and handed it to her. I said, "Hey, read this email to me. Just as you see it."

She proceeded to read the email to me and her voice rose and fell in excitement, just as she'd written it.

I said, "Okay. Now I'm going to read it back to you, just as I see it."

I read the same email, but in an angry tone—because exclamation points can be taken very different ways. I then asked, "How did that sound?"

"Angry," she replied. "Definitely not how I intended. I just wanted to come off as nice."

She'd gotten my point. The overuse of very expressive or emotional annotations in emails usually leads to more interpretation than we'd intended. Using exclamations only when you are exclaiming helps the reader best interpret the marks and the overall message.

Secondly, while she intended to come off nice, she came overly nice to a point where one might conclude she'd be a pushover. In business-to-business sales, when a customer smells a pushover, it's like a shark smelling blood.

It was a valuable lesson for her and she changed the content of her emails from then on.

The point is to just *make* the point in your emails. Keep it simple. Before you hit *send*, consider your audience and your state of mind. Practice basic email etiquette. Re-read your email at least a few times to make sure it makes sense and check for grammar and spelling errors. And when in doubt, you can always just pick up the phone.

RULE #22: LEARN THE BUSINESS & THE COMPANY

#trendawareness

#research

#entrepreneurialthinking

#criticalthinking

#dedication

Getting a promotion is a great goal and is the goal of most ambitious young professionals. I admire your ambition and totally support having a vision for your career. However, your first goal as a newly-minted professional should be to learn your job. Your second goal should be to learn the company. Your third goal, to learn the industry. You will likely learn these simultaneously and learning them will make learning anything else a lot easier.

LEARNING YOUR JOB

Believe it or not, sometimes people are put in roles just to learn. It wasn't until my third role at F&B that I realized this was happening to me. The people who'd hired me never intended for me to be the best frontline manager in the company. They'd hired me to learn, perform well, yes, and see if I had the high potential to do more. It just so happened that I did, so for the next several roles, I was there to learn and add value to further demonstrate my capabilities. I don't want to sound like performance wasn't an expectation, because it was. It just wasn't the *only* expectation after I'd proven I could get results. There was one role in which I didn't get the desired results at all, yet, I was promoted. Why? Because they'd already seen my capabilities in other areas. I simply needed to get the critical experience.

Could this be you one day? Sure, it can! But let's start by demonstrating that you can perform in this role first—and that starts with learning it in and out.

If this is a people-management role or a customer-facing role, the first three months should be spent getting to know your people and/or your customers.

For your team members, you'll want to acquire answers to questions like:

- What does their job specifically entail?
- How does your job and work impact theirs?
- What tools/resources do they rely on and what are their purposes?
- What particular support do they need from you now and on an ongoing basis?

- Who do they rely on to successfully do their job?
- What do they define as a good leader?
- What are their strengths, weakness, opportunities and threats?
- What do they enjoy outside of work?

For your customers:

- What products/services do they sell?
- How do they market those products/services?
- What is their most profitable product/service?
- What are their expectations of suppliers or the companies they support?
- What metrics (for B2B) or qualities (for B2C) matter most?
- How do the individuals with whom you do business define success? (B2B)
- What has their experience been like with your brand and role in the past? What has worked well? What hasn't?
- How does the individual or company define success in our partnership?
- What are their strengths, weaknesses, opportunities and threats?
- What do they enjoy outside of work?

For yourself:

- Who are my key stakeholders—those who can affect or be affected by my actions, behaviors, policies etc.? How is success defined in this role?

- Whom do I report to directly? Whom do I report to indirectly?

- What are my key job responsibilities?

- What metrics am I accountable to attain and where do we stand now?

- How does my job impact the jobs of others?

- How do the jobs of others impact/feed mine directly? Indirectly?

- What are the top three things I need to focus on over the next 90 days? 180 days? First year?

- What is the strategic plan for the department or team I am on for this year?

- What role do I play in the overall success of the company?

Lots of questions right? Yes. Learning your job is more than just learning what programs to use and how to execute them. You must truly understand your role, how it functions, it's role in the broader scope, your team and your customers. So how long should it take you to learn your job? At minimum it will take a year. Where managing people are involved, I would say 18 months. In fact, many companies require you to be in a role for a minimum of 18 months before they will consider you for promotion.

LEARNING THE COMPANY AND ITS BUSINESS

I've mentioned this before, but one of the things that attracted me most to the role I initially took when joining F&B Company was that it required me to learn the route system, the foundation of the company, from the ground up. The route system, which the industry used to direct store delivery, was the bloodline of F&B Company. It was literally how the product we were selling reached our customers. Without the routes, marketing wasn't necessary, production wasn't necessary, the supply chain wasn't necessary, finance wasn't necessary, etc. Not only was that automatic job security, but I was learning the most important side of the business. That would make me valuable in just about any other function in the company! Interfacing with our customers every day and the women and men who directly sold our product gave me a perspective from which any part of the company could benefit.

Learning the route system was a huge part of learning the company. I learned which were our most profitable items and why we promoted certain brands over others. I learned the secret to the company's profitability. I learned about the company's competitors and where we differed. I learned which marketing strategies worked in-store and which didn't. I learned what made for an executable sales promotions and what didn't. I learned so much. I could go on and on about it.

Once you get a handle on your job, your next job is to learn how the company works. You should be able to answer questions like:

- What is the company's culture? What are the do's and don'ts?

- What are the unwritten rules of things like communication, managing company resources, hierarchy, etc.?

- What is the primary objective of the company? How does the company measure success?

- How is the organization structured? (Org Chart)

- Who is the company's CEO and what do they care most about?

- How does the company make money?

- Which parts of the business are most profitable?

- Who are the company's strongest competitors? How are we different?

- What is the company's mission statement?

- What is the company's strategic plan for this year?

- What are the different departments/ functions of the company? What are their priorities?

- Are there sister companies? What do they do and how do they relate to our company?

- What are our strengths, weaknesses, opportunities and threats?

Not only is this stuff great to know and understand, but being curious about how the business works is attractive to leaders because it shows you care. It earmarks you as someone who has potential—seeking to learn how the whole car works, not just the engine.

LEARNING THE INDUSTRY

Do you want to be just an employee, or do you want to be an asset? Employees provide great value to the company through their work. Assets add value to the company through their knowledge. In other words, the more you know, the more valuable you are, and that knowledge doesn't have to the pertain to your role or the company. Having knowledge about your industry or function is just as valuable, if not more valuable, than learning your role and company. You should also seek to learn how the business itself works.

Learning the industry you are in means discovering the answers to questions like:

- What are the most prevalent trends in my industry?
- What are some of the outside factors impacting the industry right now?
- Who are the industry's dominant players?
- What technological advancements are being developed which might impact my industry?
- What is the future of my industry?
- What are the top three publications covering news of my industry?
- Who is on the move in my industry?

- What other industries directly influence mine?

I will be the first to admit I sucked at this when I was in Corporate America. I told myself it was because I was too busy, but the truth was, I just wasn't all that interested. Hopefully you are, though, because knowing what's going on in your industry will make you a better, more valuable asset to the company.

WAYS TO LEARN

You are probably thinking "That's a lot of questions! Where am I supposed to learn the answers to all of that!?" There are many ways you can discover answers to the above questions and others to learn your role, company and industry. Here are a few:

- **Online**- LinkedIn is such an amazing tool. If you don't have an active profile yet, you need to go get one now. Amongst a slew of other things, it will allow you to choose which industries and companies you would like to get updates on via your newsfeed or trending topics. This is a great place to learn about the industry and company.

- **Intranet**- Large organizations have an intranet to which only employees have access. It contains company-specific information, news, reports, etc. This is a great one-stop shop to learn more about both the company and industry, through the company's lens.

- **Publications**- Business journals, industry magazines and industry-driven books are all publications you could check out to learn more about your industry and company.

- **More Experienced Leaders**- These people can be mentors, more experienced colleagues, your boss or others. Ask questions of them. Of everyone! It may possibly be annoying, but my grandmother used to tell me, "If you never ask, you'll never know." At F&B, I relied heavily on more tenured Account Managers who a) didn't have any direct reports, b) had been in the business a long time and had witnessed a lot of things and c) had 20-years-worth of complaining to get out! Go to lunch with some of these veterans and "listen to your elders." You will find a wealth of knowledge and wisdom you can't find anywhere else.

Elevator Questions - I am positive you've heard of an elevator pitch by now (and if you haven't, the next chapter will help), but have you ever heard of an elevator question? Hopefully not, because I truly believe I've created the concept and am totally okay taking credit for it right now.

Similar to an elevator pitch—a brief synopsis of who you are and what you do that you should have ready on the fly—an elevator question is a thought-provoking question you should have ready on the fly to ask of anyone you come across. Like elevator pitches, elevator questions will vary based on your audience, but here are a few I've found to be effective:

o   What keeps you up at night? What are you concerned about?

o   From your perspective, what makes this company great?

o   Who is our stiffest competitor in your eyes and why?

o   Why did you choose this company?

o   How does the company define success?

o   [insert question about a role or team specific problem you are experiencing]

These types of questions are great to ask a senior leader in an elevator, hence the name, and will also make you standout. When you get in the presence of someone with authority, you should have a question ready that would answer a problem for you and your team, and for the company as a whole, or help them remember you.

KNOW YOUR STUFF

Most employees don't walk around with an encyclopedia of the business in their heads. When asked, most aren't able to blurt out answers to the questions we've mentioned in this chapter. But what if you did? How would that separate you from your peers, and what sort of impression would that give others about you?

I encourage you to view this from the vantage point of your superiors. If I was your boss and I sat down to talk to you, and you told me that you just read in the news that our company was buying out another company and there could be an opportunity for us to expand a certain department—it would immediately elevate my perception of you. People begin to see you as a leader when you can think beyond your position, when you know what the CEO of the company knows and you start thinking like an intrapreneur.

People are listening—and what you ask, or don't ask, matters. Asking the right questions, being inquisitive and knowing the company (and industry), not just your role, is important for moving your career forward. Many of the senior people you come across could have a direct or indirect say-so in your career progression. One of the things you'll always want them to be able to say about you is that you can see the big picture. You're inquisitive, you think big, you demonstrate the capability to stretch and you're well-formed. Learn your role, the business and your industry and this statement will be about you.

RULE #23: NETWORK....GENUINELY

#networking
#emotionalintelligence
#relationshipmanagement
#personalbranding

Like most people, when I thought about *networking*, I imagined shaking hands, giving out business cards to tons of strangers and walking away not remembering anything about them. It felt like a chore. And I wasn't good at it.

Even several years into my career, I thought networking was only for extroverts. The way I saw it, I didn't have a lot in common with the much older white men in my industry, so there wasn't a lot on which to connect. So I was uncomfortable even trying. During one of my yearly career-development conversations with my boss, I brought this up. I told him I was intimidated even by the thought of networking. He recommended a book called *Never Eat Alone* by

Keith Ferrazzi, and it caused a paradigm shift in the way I viewed networking.

Now I see networking less as a task, and more as an opportunity to give to someone else. That's actually what I mean when I say to network genuinely. I mean to look at networking as an opportunity to genuinely help someone else. Let me explain.

Have you ever given to someone in need? It feels good, right? You walk away with your head held high and feeling like a better human being. I encourage you to think about networking the same way. When you're speaking to someone, listen with the intent of helping. Get to know them and find out what their needs or goals are. And while you're listening, ask yourself—how can I leverage what I have to help this person? Not only does this give you the opportunity to help, but it increases your retention of information, because you're listening with an active listening ear, instead of the usual passive ear that finds conversation cumbersome.

For instance, say you meet a junior associate at an accounting firm at a holiday party. He isn't complaining, but he's telling you all about his experiences and the challenges of working at a new firm. You happen to know a director at the firm he works at who was actually an old mentor of yours. You might say, "Hey do you know so-and-so? Would you like me to introduce you to her? I think she'd be a great resource as you transition."

Chances are, he'll say, "Absolutely!"

You've just given something—a piece of your network—to someone in need, someone who can benefit from having it. Now, follow through with that and make the introduction.

At my organization, the Center for Next Generation Leadership & Professional Development, we define networking as: **cultivating meaningful relationships that add value.** That's what networking is all about—adding value to others.

It isn't altruism, it's common sense. What happens when someone gives you something? Naturally, you want to return that favor, right? Once you help someone in a professional context, they will be looking to return the favor. By helping, you are creating a circle of value, cultivating meaningful relationships instead of just shaking 50 random strangers' hands and handing out business cards.

A lot of people see networking events as a waste of time because everyone is just there to get something and nobody is there to give. What if you were at a networking event and you came across like you were actually listening and engaged—it's refreshing! It would help you stand out.

I teach a workshop/course on networking for professionals through the Center and I get one question a lot, particularly from young professionals, so I will go ahead and tackle it. What if you don't feel you have anything to give? Everybody has something. Whether that's encouragement, a piece of advice, a book recommendation or even just a smile. It's less about the value of the gift and more about the intention of going into a social situation and actively engaging to form a real connection. Sometimes, even just listening to someone for 15 minutes is a gift!

If you're shy, this approach to networking will definitely alleviate some anxiety for you. It takes the burden off of you to be an all-star networker and to just look for ways to help.

In networking situations, remember quality trumps quantity. If you make one or two meaningful connections, you've succeeded. Three is a good goal, and five at most. You don't want to be the person in the room shoveling business cards at people. It is better to make two or three real connections than 30 fly-by introductions no one will remember.

NETWORKING IS KEY

You may be thinking— is networking really that important? If I do my job well, shouldn't that be enough?

My response is—absolutely not! Networking is essential for career progression and sometimes even achieving business results. After your initial job, while performance is necessary, I would argue that networking is the key to getting future jobs and promotions. It is estimated that up to 70-85% of jobs are filled through networking and 70% of jobs aren't even posted.[1] That means many times, jobs aren't even posted, and when they are, there is likely, although not always, an identified candidate. Networking is one way you become that identified candidate.

Networking falls into the *social skills* area of emotional intelligence, which is essentially about your proficiency in managing and building relationships with people.

Table 23.1

		Self To achieving objective	Social To achieving objective
Recognition Who I Am		**Self-awareness** the ability to recognize & understand your moods, emotions, drives, and their effect on others	**Social Awareness** the ability to understand the emotional makeup of others; skill in treating people according to their emotional reactions (empathy)
Regulation What I Do		**Self-management** the ability to control or redirect disruptive impulses and moods; the propensity to suspend judgement– to think before acting	**Social Skills** Proficiency in managing relationships & building networks; an ability to find common ground & build rapport

Allow me to share a few stats that point to the importance of emotional intelligence as it relates to career.[2]

- 90% of high-performers have high emotional intelligence (EQ)
- EQ is responsible for 58% of job performance
- People with high EQ make $29k more annual

If you want to be a high-performer who is compensated like a high-performer, emotional intelligence, which networking is a part of it, will be vital, making networking vital!

If you're in sales or business development, networking is king when it comes to business results. Statistics show that business from referrals closes 70% of the time.[3] To put that in perspective, the average closing rate across industries is 19%.

The third reason networking is important is it is an essential part of one of the four components of emotional intelligence, which we covered in Rule #17.

NETWORKING TIPS

- **Have your elevator pitch ready**- an elevator pitch is a quick, persuasive synopsis used to provide an explanation of something (in this case, you). It is usually about 30 seconds long and consists of more information than a business card but a lot less information than a resume. Have an elevator pitch about yourself prepared and ready to fire off when asked, "What do you do?" or, "Tell me about yourself."

- **Use your charm**- Charm isn't a bad thing. I've used my charm many, many times in networking situations and I make no apologies for it. Using your charm is simply using your natural aura and friendly presence to make people feel comfortable. As a woman, it is much easier for me to charm men and I'd imagine it is easier for men to charm women. It is important to note that being charming and being flirtatious are two very different things. Charm and charisma go hand-in-hand and charisma is an evident characteristic of an executive presence.

- **Have a goal, not a motive**- There is nothing wrong with networking with a purpose in mind. In fact, I encourage strategic networking. However, I would encourage you to have a goal, not a motive. The truth is, in business environments, we all have some level of ulterior motive. Even when I'm looking to give, I'd like for there to be something in return. It's okay to have an end goal in mind when developing a relationship with someone, but never lead with that or expect it. We all have that. Establish the relationship first instead of immediately trying to get something from them.

In some industries, being direct is good and sometimes necessary, like the entertainment industry in L.A. as an aspiring actress, or a startup CEO looking for investors. In rare occasions like this, revealing the motive for making the connection with someone right up front may be advantageous.

- **Remember and use names**- Remembering and using someone's name whom you just met in conversation is memorable and speaks volumes to those with whom you are networking.

- **Research attendees, where possible**- This kind of goes back to that strategic relationship piece. Researching attendees before you go to a networking event can be extremely helpful in helping you prepare for potential conversations and identifying precisely whom you'd like to connect with and why.

- **Have business cards**- Make sure you have plenty of business cards with you before a networking event. However, never lead with them. Save them until the end of the conversation you are having with someone. Pitch the idea of staying in touch. Always ask for their cards, too! You can't control whether or not someone follows up with you but you can definitely control whether you follow up with them.

- **Get social**- Networking isn't always in person. According to statistics, 50% of LinkedIn members have found a job through a mutual connection and 35% of professionals say that a casual conversation on LinkedIn Messaging has led to a new opportunity.[4] Networking online can often be just as powerful as networking in person, if done consistently. LinkedIn comes in handy for anyone, but particularly salespeople, recruiters and B2B entrepreneurs. You can use it to see what your customers are engaging with, what they're liking and commenting on or what's happening in the news with their organizations. You can then intelligently converse about their company or business interests. You can even check in to see what your boss is engaging with on LinkedIn so you have a "cheat sheet" in terms of what to talk about at your next outing with her or him.

MENTORS AND SPONSORS

It is important to have mentors as a part of your network, as I'm sure you know. But how do you approach someone for mentorship? I get this question a lot. Some mentor relationships will be formally established, while others are informal.

Some people become your mentor rather naturally. You don't ask them, they just become that figure in your life over time. You find yourself calling them for guidance and advice and they love giving it to you. On the contrary, there are formal mentorship relationships that are either initiated by the mentee, the mentor or some sort of third party. That third party could be HR, your boss, another mentor or another trusted authority. You receive the same guidance and advice from this person as you would an informal mentor, but there may be some sort of structured approach to the relationship and the subjects you talk about.

If you're approaching a potential mentor yourself, a good way to start is by saying, "I think you are where I want to be one day, and I aspire to have a career path similar to yours. Would you have time to meet with me?"

When you do set up a meeting, be very thoughtful of their time, request no more than an hour, be on time and be prepared. A regular cadence for meeting with mentors is generally once a month.

Also, keep in mind, a mentor is typically one level above you, maybe two. You don't need to go to the CEO and ask him/her to mentor you. I'm sure they get those sorts of requests all the time. Honestly, what can a CEO do for you right now? Unless it's a startup company and that person is two steps away from you, you should be aiming for someone a little closer to you in the chain of command.

I have six mentors. Some are formal and others are mentors and they don't even know it! Some I haven't even met in person—they're online mentors. Sometimes you can find mentorship just from reading someone's blog or their book, never even forming a relationship.

Another potential relationship that might happen while you're networking is a sponsor relationship. What is the difference between a mentor and a sponsor?

A mentor provides guidance, support and advice, whereas a sponsor advocates for you and for your advancement. The mentor helps you develop a career plan hands-on. A sponsor helps drive that career plan. They know where you want to go and can help you get there by using their power and influence. They are high up in the organization. They have a seat at the table. Their job as your sponsor is to help advance your career and get you there. A mentor will help you find your way along the path.

Table 23.2

	Mentor	**Sponsor**
Level	1 level up	2 or more levels up
Provides...	guidance, support and advice	advocacy and opportunity
Helps...	mentee develop career plan	protégé drive career plan
Focused on...	personal & professional development of mentee	career advancement of protégé
Sought for...	navigating organization, understanding unwritten rules & culture, determining career path, assessing strengths & opportunities	career strategy and strategic placement, key relationships with people of high influence

Similar to mentorship relationships, sponsorship relationships can be formed formally and informally.

Someone once asked me, "Why would someone sponsor someone? What's in it for them?" Maybe it's because you've proven your abilities and your value to the organization and they know you're capable of doing more, possibly even one day leading the organization. As leaders, you are responsible for succession planning, which is pretty much planning who gets what role when people vacate current roles for one reason or another. Sponsoring high-potential individuals is often a part of successfully executing succession plans.

At F&B Company, there weren't very many women of color in senior leadership. To improve the bleak metrics, the company created an internal program to expedite the growth and readiness of women of color they found to be leaders with high potential. You were nominated a few levels up, and if the powers that be agreed, you became part of a formal sponsorship program. They had an obvious goal—to increase retention of their minority female talent and increase representation.

Sponsors can exist in the corporate world, the non-profit arena, the world of startups— everywhere. They can be in your company, in your city, in your industry or none of the above. The fact is, they make room for you where you want to go and are invested in your success. Identifying people like this is a great reason to get out there and network!

LEVERAGING YOUR NETWORK

In the corporate world, I've definitely used my network for many things. However, a strong network isn't just good for getting promotions. In many instances, networking is the lifeline of people's businesses. As an entrepreneur, it is definitely that for me. As a businesswoman, it's all about who you know and who knows you. Did you catch that? When people know you—versus you knowing people—therein lies influence.

One quick story and I'll get off of my networking soap box.

When I was at F&B Company, I started building my network early, even before I needed it. Building relationships is like managing money in the bank. You want to make enough of a deposit up front so when you do need to make a withdrawal, the funds are there.

The first couple of years, I was a frontline sales manager. I didn't need to worry about product getting to the warehouse—I just needed to worry about it getting out of the warehouse and into our customers' stores.

However, through many avenues, my participation in ERGs being one of them, I started developing relationships with people at the plants and the members of the over-the-road team. At the time, I built relationships with people all up and down the supply chain simply because I wanted to. I didn't know I would one day need them.

When I got to my next role in the company, I managed the people and financial processes for a larger team. When my boss became ill, it was then my job to take on the high-level sales and customer problems, if any. For a time, we had a problem getting over-the-road trucks to one of our facilities in South Carolina. Because of the way the route system was there, if those over-the-road trucks didn't come every night to make deliveries to that facility, my route salespeople wouldn't have any product to sell the next day (a serious problem for many reasons). It was getting really bad, costing us money, morale and our reputation with our customers.

To get the problem solved, I got on the phone and called folks all along the supply chain that I'd developed relationships with via networking. I had a conversation at one level, and when it didn't move the needle, I had another at the next level. That continued on until we began to see improvements. The moral of the story is I made connections with people in the beginning, before I needed to make use of them. Then when the time came, I wasn't sitting around complaining. I had relational "deposits" with everyone in the supply chain and they were inclined to help me, not just because I was their customer, but because they knew me and they wanted me to succeed.

RULE #24: GET INVOLVED, GIVE BACK

#serviceorientation

#worklifebalance

#servantleadership

#inspiring

While you are where you are to do a job, it is important to remember that you aren't there JUST to do a job. As an employee of the company, and furthermore a member of mankind, we are called on to be of service wherever possible. It is not just about collecting a check and living our best lives. We should, as gainfully employed and fortunate individuals, seek to give back. It is the right thing to do.

Not only is getting involved in initiatives outside of those that impact you and/or giving back the right thing to do, it will make you a better leader and set you up for future opportunities for advancement.

THE RIGHT THING TO DO

Not everyone is as blessed as you, my friend. You have this awesomely paying job, food on your table, clothes on your back, running water, a place to sleep at night and even some disposable income with which to enjoy life. You shouldn't feel bad for having those things, but you should be open and willing to give back wherever possible, for it is simply the right thing to do.

Many people never give back or get involved, not because they don't want to, but because they're never asked to. You may not ever be asked to give back by way of your money, time, talents, etc. at your company, so I am asking you now. Please consider lending yourself to larger initiatives that impact the greater good in your workplace or in your world. Servant leadership doesn't start and stop with our team members. We should seek to serve our fellow woman and man wherever we go.

A BETTER LEADER

Said simply—the greatest leaders are well-rounded individuals. If you look at most of our past presidents and other influential leaders, their resumes aren't one-sided. It takes far more than that to get elected and trusted by such a diverse body of people. Parts of the leader must appeal to masses of people with different backgrounds, beliefs and expectations. They don't have to be good at everything, but they must be good at far more than one thing.

Remember when you were in high school and preparing to apply for college? Just having good grades wasn't enough for a solid college application, right? You had to demonstrate that you were a well-rounded individual who could add to the college or university in ways beyond academic. You had to show volunteer experience, leadership experience and sometimes work experience. The same applies when seeking promotions at work. A well-rounded resume of leadership capabilities goes a long way.

Interacting with groups of people who aren't your peers or supervisors and still being able to lead and influence them—that speaks volumes! It's one thing to be an effective leader to your subordinates, but it's a completely different thing to influence the decisions of people who have no relation to you whatsoever.

A STRONGER REPUTATION

Think about the most successful students you knew in school. The Student Body President, the Captain of the Football team, the person voted Most Likely to Succeed. What were some of the things they did? What were they most known for? How did they show up around campus? Hopefully you can say they were highly-involved. And the last thing you remember about them was their GPAs. Amazingly, memorable people are more than their performances. They actually leave an impact and their reputation often precedes them.

Your reputation, also known as your brand, will precede you in the workplace, as we've discussed throughout this book in so many different ways. You want your brand to be positive. And producing beyond the confines of your job will lead to that. Think about it. If you are able to show you are good at your job, how does your boss and the powers-that-be know that you're truly able to do anything more than that? Giving back and/or getting involved around the company demonstrates an ability to stretch beyond your job task and do more. It builds your network outside of your immediate work group and helps establish a positive reputation within that network.

HOW TO GET INVOLVED OR GIVE BACK

So what exactly do I mean by *getting involved* and/or giving back at work? There are many ways you can do either, but a few direct examples that come to mind are serving as a mentor to newcomers, joining an ERG (employee resource group), leading a community service project or even serving as a reverse mentor to a Baby Boomer peer or manager. Let's closely look at a few ways to give back.

Join an ERG

Does your company have Employee Resource Groups (ERGs), sometimes referred to as affinity groups? These are groups of employees who join together in their workplace based on shared characteristics or life experiences. ERGs are generally based on providing support, enhancing career development and contributing to personal development in the work environment for underrepresented groups in the workplace—like women, ethnic minorities or LGBTQ community members. Most large-scale companies have several of these, presenting a very simple, turnkey way to get involved. Become an active member, get on the board, help set up for an event, volunteer to be the secretary and take notes during meetings or help with the marketing. There is no shortage of work to be done within these ERGs, so I'm sure you and your skillset will be welcomed.

At F&B Company, I was part of the black employee resource group, the women's employee resource group, and the women of color employee resource group. Through these groups, we supported different initiatives with non-profit partners in the community and also hosted professional development sessions for members. We'd do canned food drives for Thanksgiving or spend a day at the local women's shelter on a random day of the year. Being part of these groups was not only satisfying but it was professionally productive. The relationships I was able to build with people I didn't work with often made it easier to build a network and a reputation around the company. Those relationships took me far into my career.

Over time, these groups also became a safe space for me—a place where I could share concerns and/or frustrations with others who were similar to me. I found mentors and even sponsors in these groups. My fellow members definitely helped me through some tough times.

You may not be a part of an underrepresented community, and that is quite all right. **You can still join!** These groups are not exclusive. I'm sure I can speak for the Diversity & Inclusion leaders of your company and say that the purpose of these groups is actually to be the exact opposite of that—to be inclusive. Don't shy away from being a part just because the group doesn't look like you. If you support the mission and vision of the group, join in to make it a reality. See it as an opportunity to stretch yourself and learn. Listen to the conversations and seek opportunities to help. Be an ally. We had only one white person in our local black employee resource group and he was welcomed with open arms. He was active, supportive and he stood out. He attended events, learned, listened, and contributed. He used his skill set to help advance the initiatives of the ERG and as a result, he was respected as a leader amongst ALL of his peers. And all because he decided to stretch himself into a place of momentary discomfort.

If your company doesn't have any ERGs for you to join, search and ask around for similar groups within your industry. I was a part of a women's organization designed to support women in the consumer packaged goods industry. It wasn't company specific, but industry specific. Local events were held once per month and a national conference was held at least once per year in a different city every year. There are similar organizations for engineering industries, accounting, journalism, retail, etc. A quick Google search or a talk with a mentor should help get you started.

Another option if an ERG doesn't already exist in your workplace is to suggest starting one, with the help of some peers, mentors and sponsors! Talk about leaving a mark! You'll be a rock star.

Be an Activist

There are so many societal issues and civil causes we all want to fight for in today's world. Everything from racial discrimination to LGBTQ rights, to women's rights to human rights. In some cases and in some companies, this may be seen as taboo or inappropriate to discuss at work. It certainly was in our Baby Boomers' day. You simply didn't bring activism to work. However, I believe things are changing, thanks to our generation requiring more out of companies than former generations. As young leaders, we genuinely seek purpose and want to do meaningful work we are passionate about. We don't want to leave our purpose at the front steps of the office for the sake of a paycheck. 60% of Millennials say a sense of purpose is part of the reason they chose to work for their current employer. The statistic for Baby Boomers in their "Millennial age frame" doesn't exist, but I would guess it is far lower. In those days, most people worked to take care of their families. Some were lucky enough to fulfill their passion while doing it, but not 60%. The priority was different. Today, however, we want to make a difference in the world and we want to work for companies that are doing the same. If companies aren't, we will leave.

Let's face the facts. We spend about 25% of our waking lives at work. To spend a quarter of our lives not making the changes we want to see in the world is not something we want to do. Imagine the impact we can make if we channeled just 1% of that 25% fighting for social issues we care about. How much of a difference could we make if we were real-life activists on the job?

Many people think being an activist only consists of being on the front lines of protests or standing at the top of the stairs of capitol buildings and delivering powerful speeches. Those types of activists are beautiful souls, but there are other ways to activate. The definition of an *activist* is much broader. An activist is a person who makes an intentional action to bring about social or political change. You can be an activist right at your job, and I'm going to walk you through how it's done.

How to become an activist at work:

The number one way you can become an activist at work is to LEAD. Instead of complaining about the lack of opportunities to discuss real world problems, create the opportunities.

The freedom you enjoyed in college to give a voice to your passion can be transitioned into the workplace, you just have to know how within the cultural confines of your workplace. This is where your leadership *around the job* really comes in. If the opportunity for you to create social change doesn't exist within your workplace, **create it yourself!**

Of course, there are right ways and very wrong ways of doing this, and that will vary based on the culture of your specific workplace. However, I think the process holds true.

1. **Research.** First, before you launch any type of initiative, make sure your social cause aligns with the mission statement or social responsibility objectives of your company. Make sure you can explain and properly articulate this alignment,

as this will help you get organizational buy-in as you seek to accomplish your goals.

2. **Prepare/Ideate.** Spend some time brainstorming ways you can impact change concerning your social cause within the organization or with the help of the organization. Consider your company culture when ideating! For instance, holding a Black Lives Matter rally in the cafeteria might NOT fit into the average corporate culture. But an open forum on the challenges of being a minority in your city very well could.

Here are some ideas to get your wheels turning—

- Create "safe space" markers/stickers around your cause, signaling safe spaces to have tough conversations.

- Lead an open discussion/town hall meeting around your social cause.

- Start a speaker series providing perspective on social issues. (And yes, I'm available to speak! ☺)

- Start a book club reading books that shed light on your social issue. For example, if racism is your social issue, *The New Jim Crow* by Michelle Alexander is an amazing book to dive into. Perhaps you could invite Michelle to speak at your speaker series afterwards.

3. **Have an open conversation about your social cause/ passion with your manager.** Share your feelings and why this topic is so important to you. Next, share the alignment

of the cause with the organization's mission. (See Step One.) Lastly, share your ideas and get their suggestions on next steps.

4. **Gain alignment on moving forward with one or more of your ideas.** Who are the powers-that-be whose buy-in you will need to move forward? It could be HR, a Diversity & Inclusion council, the next level of management, etc. This direction will ultimately come from your manager. Prepare to present your ideas to these powers-that-be. Speak in their language. While a business case should not be necessary in discussion of morality, you are speaking to business people who likely have not done such things. Therefore, have a business case prepared. Business cases answer the question, *What is in it for them or the company?* Show your passion while presenting and explain how you will accomplish your idea while maintaining job performance.

Things to consider before you take these four steps and become an activist at work:

- **Seek employee resource groups who might already support the initiative you're passionate about and join them.** For example, let's say your social justice passion lies in seeking equal rights for women and your company has an employee resource group for women. Instead of recreating the wheel, join forces with that ERG and execute you plan together.

- **Be ready for the time commitment.** This will likely be outside the scope of your normal job, so make sure you have the time and energy to commit to leading in this space. It will likely call for hours outside of your nine-to-five.

- **Be prepared for pushback and remain calm.** There will be people who disagree with your cause or believe it is inappropriate for work. Be prepared to converse with those individuals but DO NOT lose your cool. Stay level-headed and professional. Not everyone will share your passion or understand. That doesn't mean you aren't walking the right path.

- **Remember you are still at work.** Radicalism will not work and is not acceptable. Be tactful, professional and strategic. Being an activist at work should ADD to the value you bring as an employee, not take away from it.

- **Don't get caught up in the numbers.** I'm a firm believer that you change the world one person at a time. If you can increase awareness and enlightenment around your cause by just one person, you have made progress.

- **You are taking a risk.** In some companies, this is uncharted territory. No one else has had the guts to do this, to this degree. Everyone else played it safe and upheld the line between work and changing the world. You are different. You are taking a risk. More likely than not, your actions will be praised, but there is a possibility that it can stunt your growth, that it can blacklist you. I want you to be fully aware of this possibility before you start down this path. But if you're passionate about your social cause—it is likely worth it.

It may seem crazy to some that I am proposing the idea of being an activist at work. They, especially our more experienced and conservative professionals, may think this is neither the proper place nor the proper time. That it will interfere with job performance. To those people I would ask—where is the proper place to address and challenge the prevalent social issues of the world in which we all live and do business? When is the proper time to make real changes in our world? Being an activist at work is a great way to get involved, show leadership capabilities outside of your direct reports and lead a purposeful professional life. It comes with risks though, my friend.

Some causes you may get behind could be raising awareness around a certain illness that is near to your heart, clean water initiatives, racial justice, world hunger, women's rights, the gender pay gap, LGBTQ rights, homelessness in your city, economic mobility in your city, affordable housing, K-12 literacy and more. Causes you probably want to steer clear of (in traditionally corporate environments) would include anything pertaining to partisan politics or religion.

Be A Mentor

You may think because you're so new in your career and to the organization that you don't have much to offer as a mentor. You'd be completely wrong! Regardless of how new you are, there will soon be someone newer, if there isn't already, and they could probably benefit from hearing your perspective. Think about it. It's great to be mentored by someone with decades of experience and proven results, as they can coach you to long-term success. However, the process you're going through now is probably very different than it was when they went through it. The technology is undoubtedly different, making the job itself—along with expectations and responsibilities—very different. For that reason, it would also be beneficial to be mentored by someone who recently went through the process and can provide advice on being successful in the short-term. Both are important and you, as a newer employee, would be a great candidate for the latter type of mentor.

So what does becoming a mentor to someone with less experience than you look like? Simply serving as a resource for them when needed. That could consist of being a sounding board, providing feedback on specific deliverables, answering questions they may be afraid to pose to more senior staff, aiding in project deliverables, etc. It does not have to be a formal relationship by any means. You do, however, want to make sure you mention it in your performance reviews, often conducted at the middle and end of the year. The point is to get involved, but remember one of the results of getting involved is building a stronger reputation. You can't do that if no one knows about it.

Another type of mentorship you are perfect to be a part of is reverse mentoring. Reverse mentoring is when older leaders, most times executives, are paired with and mentored by younger employees to build their capabilities in topics such as technology, social media and current trends. Think about it. A Baby Boomer executive probably knows the business inside and out. They are FAR more skilled than you in just about everything pertaining to the business except for the newer initiatives driving the business and our world today. You are better at operating technology, navigating social media and understanding social and cultural trends of your generation. They could learn a lot from you and many are open to doing so.

Your company may or may not have a formal reverse mentoring program, but it's worth asking about and exploring. If it doesn't exist, maybe you might consider starting one with you and an executive as the guinea pig. Unlike the prior mentorship opportunity I mentioned, this one will likely be a formalized mentorship relationship.

If you walk away with nothing else from this chapter, I want you to remember this—you don't have to be at a company for 10 years before you can make a contribution beyond your job responsibilities. You don't have to be a veteran before someone can learn from you.

And you don't have to leave your passion at the door of the office. There are ways you can incorporate the things you are passionate about and feel compelled to impact in the world right there in your cubicle. Not only will others benefit from you getting involved and giving back, but you will, too, by way of career progression.

Start now!

RULE #25: DON'T BE SO SORRY

#selfconfidence
#selfawareness
#verbalcommunication

This may seem like an unnecessary chapter, but I've actually seen this one word—*sorry*—make a difference in people's careers, particularly with young professionals. And the truth is, it impacts more women than men. Have you noticed we literally say *sorry* constantly in American culture? Maybe I see it more because I live in the south, the home of southern hospitality, but I've observed people literally apologize for apologizing! It's gotten ridiculous. It's to the point where some people will literally walk up and greet you by starting off with the word *sorry*! What has gotten into us? We've become so overly apologetic that when we are truly apologetic it can be hard to tell.

Let me further explain why something as seemingly small as this matters.

For one, it's annoying. Secondly, as a leader within your organization, it sets the wrong tone for people regarding you. Confidence has been a theme throughout this book. As a leader, you want to approach even awkward moments with confidence, with an aura that you deserve to be there despite your mistakes. When you constantly apologize, particularly for things that don't warrant an apology, people struggle putting you in a position of power in their minds.

In a team member's mind, constant unnecessary apologizing makes you look like a subdued figure with her or his head bowed down in a place of weakness. It speaks insecurity rather than confidence. It makes people question whether you can handle it when big things go wrong. Constant apologizing could send the message that you are overwhelmed or fragile. Your team may be hesitant to bring issues to you in the future and doubt your availability to support them or handle feedback.

This is particularly important for a woman in a male-dominated industry or company. There may already be an ignorant stereotype that women can't do this job and if you display your insecurities, that will only fuel the stereotype. The more they become sure that their stereotype is accurate, the harder it will become to keep their respect and maintain your position of power as the leader.

Thirdly, constant unnecessary apologizing makes people question your genuineness. Think about a marriage. If I get the same response to my husband cheating as I do for him not putting the toilet seat down in the bathroom, I may question rather he's truly sorry on the greater offense. This situation is really no different. If you are constantly apologizing for trivial things that don't matter, people may have a hard time determining if you're really sorry when they truly are owed an apology.

Lastly, constant unnecessary apologizing is self-defeating and self-deprecating behavior that could potentially be coming from a deeper place—a place we want to unlearn. Perhaps it means that we hold other's opinions and reactions in overly high regard or that we are extremely conflict-averse and we use excessive apologizing as a way to claim responsibility in order to make a problem disappear.[1] Constantly apologizing can kill your confidence and contribute to your own self-doubt. You are what you tell yourself you are. Apologizing excessively tells you that you are all the things we mentioned earlier—insecure, incapable, undeserving, etc.

Please do note, I'm not talking about genuine remorse. When you've messed up, you should definitely identify your faults and make a commitment to adjust. But I find it hard to believe you are wrong every time you apologize.

APOLOGIZE ONLY WHEN YOU MEAN IT

There is absolutely a difference between taking responsibility for your mistake and excessively apologizing. Saying you're sorry is sometimes absolutely necessary and something you should definitely do, even with your team members. Being humble enough to admit when you're wrong is an important part of being a leader. When a parent admits they did something wrong and apologizes to their child for it, I think it shows valuable vulnerability. It shows that they're not above being wrong and it demonstrates the habits they are likely teaching the child. That is a powerful thing, and frankly, the same goes for leaders. Apologizing when you are wrong helps your team see you are open to feedback and committed to consistent improvement. These things help them trust you—and it's one of the keys to effective multigenerational leadership.

Now, apologizing means nothing if you don't change the behavior—if you don't follow through. It's more meaningful and effective to apologize once and correct the behavior than constantly apologizing and continue to do the same things. *Sorry* means nothing without action.

DO'S AND DON'TS

Don't apologize for:

- **Asking for someone's time.** You're not wrong for asking for someone's time. There's no need to apologize for doing so.

- **Missing small details.** Do not apologize if you miss a small detail in a conversation or email. There are other ways to address it. Just say, "I missed that," or, "I overlooked that," and correct the issue.

- **Getting feedback.** When getting feedback from a superior, just acknowledge the error, if there is one, commit to making the necessary changes and do so. There's no need to apologize every time your manager points out how you can adjust or do something better.

- **Providing your opinion.** You have a right to your opinion and to interject it. You don't have to apologize before doing so, while doing so or after doing so.

Do apologize for:

- **Wasting people's time.** For instance, missing important meetings or major details that cost people time or money. For example, if someone drives in from out of town for a meeting with you which you completely forgot about, that warrants an apology.

- **Mistakes on behalf of your team.** As a leader, apologizing on behalf of your team is simply something you will have to do, especially if it is customer-service related. If you're in customer service, apologizing on behalf of your company or your team can quickly defuse a tense situation. As "the boss," this is often all a complaining customer wants to hear, along with a commitment to fix the problem.

- **When you mean it.** It's a sign of strength to apologize when you know you're wrong—and others know that you're wrong. Depending on the situation and where the error was made, this apology can be done privately or publicly. Public apologies show a profound amount of humility but aren't always appropriate.

DO THIS INSTEAD

Let's make a deal. You and I both are going to try HARD to remove, "I'm sorry," from our vocabularies. In order to be an effective multigenerational leader, you have to rid yourself of this apologetic demeanor. But of course I'm going to help.

Here are words or phrases you can use instead of *sorry*...

- **Thanks.** If you miss something in an email, you can say, "Thanks for flagging that," or, "Thanks for bringing that to my attention," versus "I'm sorry, I missed that detail." "Good catch!" is another option. You are praising their behavior but not demeaning yourself.

- **Forgive me.** Instead of saying "I'm sorry," particularly when the situation warrants a true apology, try saying, "Please forgive me." For example, "I completely forgot about our call today. Please forgive me."

- **I desire.** This statement puts the focus on what you wish to change in the future regarding the situation versus you feeling sorry about what has already happened. "I desire to respond in a more timely fashion in the future."

- **Pause/Breathe.** For a lot of people, sorry has become a filler word, similar to "*Uh, Um, So,*" (mine is *so*), that are used to fill space or silence while we think to finish a thought. Before you are about to say *sorry* as a filler word, breathe in through your mouth. You'll notice you can't say a word. For example, instead of, "In the past we have collected...

sorry...used coats for the local shelter," simply replace the *sorry* with a pause and/or a breath.

- **Pardon Me:** Many people apologize for interrupting someone or for asking for someone's time, especially our leaders. We too often say, "Sorry to bother you," or, "Sorry to interrupt." Instead, try simply saying, "Pardon me," or, "Excuse me." For example, "Pardon me, do you have a minute?" versus, "Sorry to bother you, do you have a minute?"

- **My Mistake:** In the case of an error on your part, "My mistake," is a good way to own the error and should be accompanied by a commitment to potentially correct and a promise to course correct the action for future reference. For example, "That is my mistake. I'll add that to the contract and shoot it back to you," versus, "I'm sorry. I meant to add that to the contract. Silly me! I will correct and send it back right away."

———⟋⟍———

At the end of it all, avoiding the word *sorry* and excessive apologizing is really about our core values throughout this book—gaining respect, earning and keeping trust and displaying confidence. Using strong, authoritative language like, "I will," instead of submissive language like, "I'm sorry," will help you achieve all three of these goals as you lead your multigenerational team and influence those around you.

———⟋⟍———

SEE IT THROUGH

#commitment

#determination

They say the first year of marriage is the hardest. The same goes for entering the professional world and becoming a leader. You will have hard days and days you'll be tempted to quit. Don't! Stay the course and see it through. Allow this experience to build character in you and mature you professionally. The lessons you learn here, in these first few years of leading people, will be the foundation for your professional future. Receive it with care and enjoy the process.

My hope, after reading this book, is that you know more now than you did when you first picked it up. If I did my job, you should have a deeper perspective on the next leadership role you step into and should be more prepared to handle the complexities of the multigenerational workplace you're leading. You should better understand what it takes to be an effective leader of a multigenerational team and have a set of tools to use as you navigate your first few years of professional leadership.

We scratched the surface on a lot between the front and back covers of this book. Some of these chapters could have been books in and of themselves. After all is said and done, this book, and all the rules therein are really about three things:

- Gaining the **respect** of those you lead
- Earning and keeping their **trust**
- Displaying **confidence** that makes you trustworthy

That is really it. Each of the 25 Rules relate back to one or more of these three principles in some fashion. Respect, Trust and Confidence. *Respect* is the love language of Baby Boomers, Gen X has to *trust* you in order to join you and Millennials and Gen Z have to have *confidence* that you're leading them somewhere worthwhile. The truth is that all three of these things matter when leading anyone, regardless of their generation. For that reason, when leading your multigenerational team, seeking to do these three things will be well worth your time and energy as they transcend the generational bounds.

If you are able to accomplish these three things as a young leader, you will be successful. But remember, being a leader in the workplace is not just about leading within your team. It is just as much about how you lead around the office. Remember to keep in mind all of your internal stakeholders—your PSS. Peers, subordinates and supervisors.

You now have a set of rules to follow to help you be successful **Before the Job, On the Job and Around the Job.** Rules that open your mind to important perspectives, rules that get you results and rules that get you promoted. If you find yourself overwhelmed by the 25 Rules or stuck in a situation without your "cheat sheet," simply ask yourself these three questions:

- **Does this decision increase or maintain the respect my PSS have for me?**
- **Does this decision uphold the trust I have built or am building with my PSS?**
- **Does this decision display healthy confidence that helps my PSS trust me?**

If the answer to at least two of the three is *yes*, you're probably making a solid decision. If you're still struggling, tap a trusted mentor, or shoot me a text or email. My response time may be slow, but don't let that deter you from reaching out. My support of your career and professional growth doesn't stop here. I'm only an email or text message away.

If you are not able to get guidance, make your move and see what the results shall be. You may make mistakes and that's okay. You won't be perfect. As we discussed in Rule #4, you will be tempted to pretend like you know everything to prove you deserve to be there. Remember the reason you're there is not because you're so great now…but because whoever hired you believed you'll be really great later.

Remember, the workplace needs you! They need your smarts, your tech savvy, your enthusiasm, your perspective, your skillset, your talents and so much more. You are valuable and as you grow, following the rules of this book and others you learn along the way, will allow you to become ever more valuable.

And you need the workplace, too. You have so much to learn as a budding professional. The good part about it is everything you need to know is out there. Learning it will be the fun part. Learn from your Boomers. Listen to your Xers. Take advice from your older Millennials and lean on your Gen Z peers. The road to success is not walked alone.

I want you to go out there and set an example of what better leadership looks like. Just by reading this book, you now know more about the unwritten rules of the workplace, and leadership, than any other group who came before you. Even if you apply just a few of these rules, you will be a better reflection on your generation. It will make me so proud to hear stories from young professionals out there who have applied all, or even some of these rules, and saw results. Please text or email me those!

Subscribe to my newsletter on my website for monthly leadership and professional development tips in video or short-text format. If you're interested in sharing these lessons with others, I would love to come speak at your company, school or association about this book or other professional development topics essential to the success of young professionals everywhere. Email info@ravensolomon.com for bookings.

If you could look one year into your future—I hope you'll see a well-rounded, professional, multigenerational workplace leader, able to navigate challenges with confidence. A leader with just as many soft skill capabilities as hard skill.

You will be great, my friend. See it through.

ACKNOWLEDGMENTS

#thankyou

To my first, second and third teams of employees in the Raleigh DC—You taught me so much. There wouldn't be a book like this without you. Thank you for your patience, your presence and your commitment to our shared vision.

To my fourth team of employees in the Greenville Zone—You received me during my most personally destitute time. You made me smile, you made me laugh and you gave me a reason to continue to show up every morning. Thank you for your #Response.

To my fifth team of employees in the Charlotte Zone—You taught me the most about leading a multigenerational team. I was so charmed by each of you in a very unique way. You made this role my favorite. Thank you for releasing me into the next stage of my life and career which eventually gave way to this book.

To my siblings, Reginald and Rochelle—Knowing you two believe I can do anything and you support me in that pursuit is literally the wind beneath my wings. Thank you for always having my back and making sure my wings don't fall too low. #rcs

To my best friend, Shakiria—I cannot remember a time without you in my life. You were the first person I told about this *Leading Your Parents* concept and you were, unsurprisingly, there every step of the way. I couldn't ask for a better BFF.

To my family—I am beyond blessed to have been born into you. You are my biggest cheerleaders and I get such joy seeing the pride on your face when WE accomplish yet another goal. You've seen me at my worst and you've helped me reach my best. I am grateful for you.

To my mentors—You've poured into me, corrected me, encouraged me, guided me and sustained me. Your presence lights the path God has purposed for me and I'm simply grateful. This book would lack so much without the depth of wisdom you've willingly shared with me over the years. Thank you.

To my writing coach, Shannon—There would be no book without you. Thank you for holding me accountable, listening to my random rambled stories and helping me make sense of it all. We did it... in time!

To my editor, Debra—Thank you for taking something good and making something great. We pulled it off!

To my pre-launch team—Tyelisa, Harrison, Shakiria, Vernisha, Darryl, Corliss, Khalia, Sherrell, Latesha, Bridell, Erica, James, Beti, Daniel and Quintel—I called you literally in the 11th hour and unsurprisingly, you answered. I'm so grateful to have people in my life like you who are willing, at the drop of a dime, to support and undergird my vision. I appreciate all that you are in my life and your contribution to make *Leading Your Parents* a success. Thank you.

To my launch team—Thank you for your commitment and dedication to helping make *Leading Your Parents* everything it can truly be. To use your social capital on my behalf means the world and I am eternally grateful.

To my Grandmother—I knew I wouldn't make it through this one without crying. You literally introduced me to scholarship, education and a world beyond what I could see. Thank you for your daily investment in my future. Without you, I never would have known I could be an author. Although my appreciation was deferred, thank you. Thank you. Thank you. Thank you.

Lastly, but certainly not least,

To my mother—This book is dedicated to you for many, many reasons. I first saw leadership through you and boy did I have an extraordinary example. I am so proud to be just like you—caring, passionate, charismatic and positive. You are my greatest role model and my everything. There is nothing I will ever accomplish that isn't in some part due to the woman you were. Not only is there no *Leading Your Parents* without you, there is no ME without you.

NOTES

Preface

1. Thomas Gailey, "The Servant Leader: Transforming Executive Style,"

   https://www.sju.edu/news-events/magazines/haub-school-review/haub-school-review-spring-2015/servant-leader-transforming

Introduction

1. World Economic Forum, "The Future of Jobs," http://www3.weforum.org/docs/WEF_Future_of_Jobs.pdf

2. Tamyra Pierce, "Social Anxiety and Technology: Face-to-face communication versus technological communication among teens,"

   https://www.sciencedirect.com/science/article/pii/S0747563209000971

3. Payscale and Future Workplace, "2016 Workforce-Skills Preparedness Report," https://www.payscale.com/about/press-releases/payscale-and-future-workplace-release-2016-workforce-skills-preparedness-report

Understanding the Generations

1. Dictionary.com,

   https://www.dictionary.com/browse/generation

2. The Center for Generational Kinetics, "The State of Gen Z,"

   https://genhq.com/

3. Lifecourse Associates, "What is a Generation?"

   https://www.lifecourse.com/about/method/phases.html

4. Pew Research Center, "Millennials Projected to Overtake Baby
   Boomers as America's Largest Generation,"

   http://www.pewresearch.org/fact-tank/2018/03/01/millennials-
   overtake-baby-boomers/

5. Workplace Trends, "The Multi-generational Workplace Study,"

   https://workplacetrends.com/the-multi-generational-
   leadership-study/

Rule #2: Value their Values

1. Adecco, "Job Stability Trumps Passion for Majority of College
   Students According to Adecco Way to Work Survey," https://
   www.adeccousa.com/about-adecco-staffing/newsroom/press-
   releases/way-to-work-survey-2015/

2. The Center for Generational Kinetics, "Gen Z is Learning from
   Millennials' Money Mistakes,"

   https://genhq.com/gen-z-2017-research-infographic-stats-
   money-saving-debt/

3. EY, "Trust in the Workplace: Generation Z Values," https://www.ey.com/gl/en/about-us/our-people-and-culture/ey-global-study-trust-in-the-workplace-study-highlights-generation-z-values

Rule #3: Communicate their Way

1. Careers and Education News, "A History of Communication," https://careersnews.ie/a-history-of-communication/

2. Forbes, "Eight ways Generation Z will Differ from Millennials in the Workplace," https://www.forbes.com/sites/deeppatel/2017/09/21/8-ways-generation-z-will-differ-from-millennials-in-the-workplace/#3702efb276e5

3. The Center of Generational Kinetics, "The State of Gen Z 2017: Meet the Throwback Generation," http://genhq.com/gen-z-2017/

Rule #5: Give a Proper Introduction

1. Goleman, Daniel, "Leadership that Gets Results," Harvard Business Review, March-April 2000 p. 82-83

Rule #7: Display Confidence

1. CNBC Make It, Ruth Umoh, "How Making Eye-Contact can Help You Appear More Confident at Work," https://www.cnbc.com/2017/08/17/how-making-eye-contact-can-help-you-appear-more-confident-at-work.html

2. Glass, Lilian, "The Body Language Advantage," Fair Winds Press, 2012.

3. Heleen Vandromme, Dirk Hermans and Adriaan Spruyt, "Indirectly Measured Self-esteem Predicts Gaze Avoidance, Self and Identity,"

Rule #10: Do the Little Things

1. Chief Executive, Stephen M. R. Covey, "The Business Case for Trust," https://chiefexecutive.net/the-business-case-for-trust/

2. Franklin Covey, "The Speed of Trust,"

   https://www.franklincovey.com

3. Dictionary.com

   https://www.dictionary.com/browse/emotional-intelligence

Rule #14 Put Down the Phone

1. New York Post, SWNS, "Americans check their phones 80 times a day: study,"

   https://nypost.com/2017/11/08/americans-check-their-phones-80-times-a-day-study/

2. Inc., John Brandon, "The Surprising Reason Millennials Check Their Phones 150 Times a Day,"

   https://www.inc.com/john-brandon/science-says-this-is-the-reason-millennials-check-their-phones-150-times-per-day.html

Rule #17: Demonstrate Presence

1. Maetrix, "Emotional Intelligence,"

   https://www.maetrix.com.au/emotional-intelligence/

Rule #21: Email with Etiquette, Text with Caution

1. Medium, Irene Rufferty, "SMS vs. Email: How Many Emails People Get Every Day," https://medium.com/bsg-sms/sms-vs-e-mail-how-many-emails-people-get-every-day-4f5987e45492

Rule #23: Network… Genuinely

1. Virgin, "Infographic: The Importance of Face-to-Face Networking,"

   https://www.virgin.com/entrepreneur/infographic-the-importance-of-face-to-face-networking

2. Talentsmart, "About Emotional Intelligence,"

   http://www.talentsmart.com/about/emotional-intelligence.php

3. Allbusiness, Jonathan Farrington, "The Power of Referral Selling,"

   https://www.allbusiness.com/the-power-of-referral-selling-14845859-1.html

4. Small Business Trends, Shubhomita Bose, "Data Shows LinkedIn's Value as a Networking, Branding Tool,"

   https://smallbiztrends.com/2017/10/linkedin-statistics-small-business.html

Rule #25: Don't be so Sorry

1. Forbes, Melody Wilding, "Stop Over-Apologizing at Work:3 Steps to Quit Saying Sorry so Much,"

https://www.forbes.com/sites/melodywilding/2016/09/06/
stop-over-apologizing-how-to-quit-saying-sorry-so-
much/#1dd2b56d1d12

INDEX

ABOUT THE AUTHOR

RAVEN SOLOMON is a millennial who's cracked the code on how to lead intergenerational teams. In *Leading Your Parents: 25 Rules to Effective Multigenerational Leadership for Millennials and Gen Z*, she shares her leadership principles and practical advice for young professionals seeking to transition into leadership positions in today's diverse workplace.

As the valedictorian of her college graduating class and one of the youngest-ever executives in the Fortune 50 company at which she spent nearly a decade, Raven has shown that her approach yields results. Her story of overcoming challenges of poverty, illness, and bullying to surpass her goals and lead through service is motivational and relatable.

Whether as a keynote speaker, author, or the founder and president of the Charlotte-based *Center for Next Generational*

Leadership and Professional Development, a startup focused on providing soft-skill development to the leaders of tomorrow, Raven uses her formidable leadership skills and business acumen to help Millennial and Gen Z professionals reach their full potential as leaders and changemakers.

When she's not writing down her trade secrets or mentoring future world changers, she's cheering on the Carolina Panthers or NC State Wolfpack, and searching for the best local eatery to check out with friends in Charlotte, NC.

» **Connect with Raven**

Instagram: raven_solo
LinkedIn: in/ravensolomon
Facebook: solomon.raven
Twitter: raven_solo
Cell Phone: (704) 266-0652

» **To book Raven** for speaking engagements or workshops, visit www.ravensolomon.com or email info@ravensolomon.

» **For more information** about the *Center for Next Generation Leadership & Professional Development*, visit www.nextgenlpd.com or email info@nextgenlpd.com.